LLOYD

AFRICA BITES
SCRAPES AND ESCAPES
IN THE AFRICAN BUSH

LLOYD CAMP CONSULTING
AFRICA

Everything's a story. Everything.
As long as it's told well.

Advice from a friend

First Printing, 2015

ISBN-13: 978-1515015987
ISBN-10: 151501598X

Published by Lloyd Camp Consulting Africa
Richmond-upon-Thames
Surrey, UK

www.lloydcamp.co.za

For Sue
> 12

Distances and weights

1 metre = 1.1 yards
1 kilometre = 0.6 miles
1 mile = 1.6 kilometres
1 kilogram = 2.2 pounds

CONTENTS

ACKNOWLEDGEMENTS

Pretty much everyone thinks they have a book in them. Very few people actually find the time or courage to write it down. I finally found both, thanks to the nudging and prodding of several very important people in my life:

My parents, Kelson and Moira Camp, who nurtured a love of the wild in me. Those family holidays at Lynn Avis, in Zululand and the Natal Drakensberg were, apart from your love, your greatest gift.

Malcolm Ainscough, who encouraged me on a desert day in Namibia to get started, persuading me that these stories are not just for the fireside at the end of a day's safari but should be appreciated by a wider audience. Thanks, Fox, for helping me to see that it was both possible and necessary to get them onto paper.

Peter Allison and Chris Bakkes for leading the way. Most of all, for their enduring friendship and incessant nagging. Here it is, boys.

The many friends, guides, clients and lodge staff with whom I have worked and adventured with over the years across Africa, and who have become part of my story.

My father, Kelson, for the sketches.

Caitlin Mackesy Davies, for turning this into a vastly better book.

Perry Rendell, who was magnificent in the technical aspects of this book: your help and friendship is immensely appreciated.

Sue, who is everything to me. Without you, none of these adventures could have happened. I love you.

Africa

The countries in which these stories take place

Southern Africa

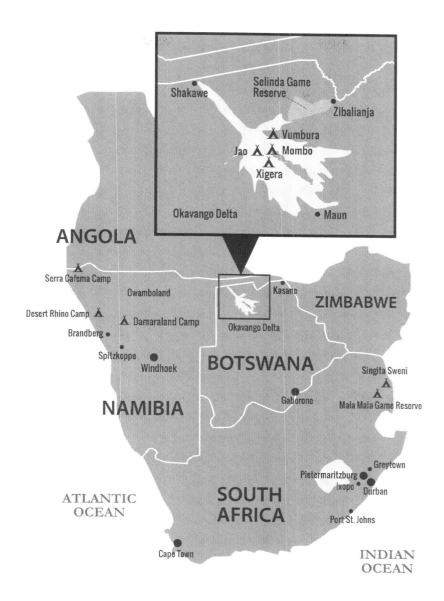

Shakawe

Selinda Game Reserve

Zibalianja

Vumbura

Jao   Mombo

Xigera

Okavango Delta

Maun

ANGOLA

Serra Cafema Camp

Owamboland

Kasane

ZIMBABWE

Desert Rhino Camp

Damaraland Camp

Okavango Delta

Brandberg

Spitzkoppe

Windhoek

BOTSWANA

Singita Sweni

Gaborone

Mala Mala Game Reserve

NAMIBIA

Greytown

Pietermaritzburg

Ixopo   Durban

ATLANTIC OCEAN

SOUTH AFRICA

Port St. Johns

Cape Town

INDIAN OCEAN

A WORD FROM MALCOLM AINSCOUGH
CHAIRMAN OF MAGALENA CORPORATION

It is a great pleasure to be invited to introduce this book to you. Lloyd's eloquent writings provide an intimate and uplifting sense of his dynamic career in our industry, often suffused with a delightful sense of humour, and always with the passion that has been the foundation of his success.

Lloyd skillfully gives fluent and objective style to the work he holds so dear and for which he is so universally respected. Over the past twenty-three years he has given great delight to thousands of our safari guests, he has changed the lives of trainee safari guides in Namibia, Botswana, Uganda and Zimbabwe, and has also founded and managed a successful staff training division within Wilderness Safaris. This book places him in the forefront of storytellers about wild animals simply because he is as interested in people as he is in wildlife.

I truly hope that this unique narrative doesn't just provide an intriguing record of a potentially vanishing world; the observation and photography of wild animals by our safari guests is simply one end-product of Lloyd's remarkable life, which has covered an extraordinary range of activities amongst the fabulous characters and creatures that surround us. In these pages this gentle, generous and admirable man has produced a platform for projecting the vast emotions created by any visit to the wilds of Africa, reminding me evocatively of the greatest of all of Hemingway's quotes: "If I have ever seen magic, it has been in Africa."

Your support of this book and our professional partnership will materially assist in the maintenance of some of the most fabulous wildlife destinations on this planet, allowing Lloyd to continuing to play his own part in the conservation of the last iconic wildlife destinations on the continent he loves so well.

INTRODUCTION

When I tell people that I lead safaris in Africa, they always ask me the same questions: what's the scariest experience you have ever had? What's the most dangerous animal in Africa? What's the closest you have ever come to death? Once, intriguingly, a young woman asked me whether I have any "legendary scars". I used to try to avoid answering these questions because I hate to promote the illusion that being a safari guide means that I walk on a daily basis on the edge of death and disfigurement. I am forever pointing out that, although as a matter of course I have indeed had terrifying moments at the hand of nature, mostly I lead a gentle and peaceful existence in the outdoors. But it seems that those are not the stories that people want to hear. When it comes to bush stories, they don't want poetry. They want peril.

I think this is because people are instinctively fascinated by fear and are attracted to those who have survived fearful situations. Personally, I avoid roller coasters and hate horror movies but many people *love* being scared by them. They undoubtedly fulfill a certain human need. For many nervous safari clients, just the act of coming to Africa, the so-called "Dark Continent", is a big leap. Safaris certainly do provide many unexpected thrills. Africa is constant living theatre. The sound of a hippo munching grass outside your tent at night can be loud and horrifying if you don't know what you are listening to. If you don't know better, every single mosquito seems certain to be about to give you malaria. Even a harmless gecko calling in your room at night can sound eerily like the slow creaking of a door, *your* door, opening. Danger and fear apparently lie everywhere, if you are out of your comfort zone. It's easy as a guide to be dismissive of these perceived fears, but of course, rational or otherwise, they are totally real to the person who experiences them. I happen to know what a hippo sounds like when it is feeding, and I love it: the difference between thrill and fear is that you *understand* thrill.

But even if you *are* reasonably comfortable in the outdoors, the simplicity of the bush can nevertheless become confusing really quickly. The gentle serenity of the wilderness can be dramatically punctuated and your day will be filled with unexpectedly bright colours. So I have come to see that these questions about Africa's perceived dangers are inevitable and natural, and *do* need to be answered.

Therefore, these short stories are indeed about the many close calls and narrow escapes that I have experienced both in the course of my career as a safari guide in Africa and in my earlier life. Honed over a thousand campfires, and told where possible in the quirky idiom of real characters, they aren't really about peril and fear, though. They are about courage and resilience and pushing through.

Throughout my life I have encountered and been inspired by many remarkable people, fellow Africans as well as safari clients from every corner of the globe, who have faced scary moments of many kinds and who have each risen to the challenge in their own way. We tend to think of fear, in an African context at least, as being harassed by a large wild animal. But actually, most fears are less obvious and more insidious than that and we all deal with them differently, sometimes magnificently. Sometimes hilariously, too.

PART I
SAFARI SCRAPES

1

ICE IN THE VEINS

Your blood runs cold. It is absolutely no exaggeration to say this. It feels like ice-cold water is suddenly pumping through your veins. It happens in a split-second.

And right now it's happening to me again.

I've experienced this dreadful feeling twice before in my life. The first time I felt unadulterated terror was as a six-year-old lad in Greytown, the small village in which I grew up, when a Doberman pinscher rushed at me through an open gate as I walked to school. I was terrified of that dog. It was there every single day, so I always used to wait for a passing adult, who I could shelter behind, to catch up to me. This day no adult came. I was alone and I had to risk it, and that dog, big and heavy, hurtled at me, barking hoarsely like some dark apocalyptic evil. I momentarily cowered in shock, then ran for my life, and the dog, his territory now secure from apparent threat, quickly gave up the chase. After that I started taking safer, more creative routes to school.

The second occasion was also at the hands of a dog, a nasty *kraal* animal from a local settlement that was asleep in the gum trees behind the old farmhouse on my grandparents' small holding. I startled it awake as I walked in the plantation, and it rose at my feet, rushing at me with raised hackles and bared teeth and a terrible low growl. Its ferocious reaction was abrupt and extreme, and the blood coursed through me like ice as I stood shocked and afraid and screaming at it. The dog backed off and I went straight home, pale, shaken and relieved.

But during neither of those incidents did I think that I was going to die.

Today, on a warm day as I paddle a small canoe on the Kunene river, I do. I am sure of it. I've always wondered how that was going to happen. It's a massive crocodile. And it's coming fast! Today, a crocodile is going to kill me. Who would have thought?

At the start of this day, I had a very different adventure in mind. Serra Cafema camp is a remote luxury safari lodge on the northern Namibian border with Angola, and I'm excited at the prospect of finding a little Cinderella Waxbill. It's a very rare bird in these parts and is featured as a special attraction in the brochure that advertises the camp. I've never been to this area before, so after lunch while everyone else is taking a siesta, I set off to investigate the riverine bush in search of the bird. No-one I know has ever seen one and I don't really know exactly where to start looking for it. Do they skulk in undergrowth, or flit from twig to twig in the open? Do they prefer dense reedbeds or open country? My Newman's Birds of Southern Africa is not very clear on this so I'll just have to scout around with fingers crossed. The problem is that I can't gain access to the low vegetation along the edge of the river where I suspect one might be lurking. But then I see a small one-man canoe in the reeds. Hallelujah! There's a silly little plastic paddle in it, pretty useless really, a child's toy, nothing more; but the waxbill awaits. I drag the boat into the water and begin paddling upstream, scanning the reeds for birds. There is an intriguing rustling in there and I clamp my binoculars, a guide's most important field tool, to my eyes, but then a sixth sense alerts me. I look up and see that I am drifting quite quickly towards the rapids just downstream from the camp. The waxbill will have to wait.

I realize that I have badly underestimated the force of the current, and I'm getting into a bit of trouble. I rapidly decide to paddle as hard as I can towards the Angolan bank and try to beach the canoe against a steep sand dune that cascades into the Kunene, there to await rescue from the camp staff once they notice my absence. But my troubles have scarcely begun.

I'm making good progress towards Angola when a movement on the surface of the water about 100 metres upstream catches my attention. Pausing in mid-stroke, I stare hard at the spot. What is it? The water there is now white, and moving, and a sudden awful certainty overtakes me.

Crocodile! And my blood freezes.

The crocodile is coursing in a long, swift curve across the river at me. The Kunene is famous for its disagreeable crocs, man-eaters that attack local Himba villagers and their livestock, dragging them under to a ghastly watery grave. The lodge manager told me all about them at lunch.

"Watch out for those bloody flatdogs, my friend. They're hellava aggressive around here. *Jislaaik*, I could tell you some stories, man!" he'd said.

But my eagerness to find the bird over-ruled any common sense. Anyway, I told myself, people love to exaggerate, especially about crocodiles. I know crocodiles; I've seen thousands of them as a guide, and been in boats on the water with them before. I had dismissed the possibility that I might be in any real danger from these Kunene ones.

But I am.

The croc has narrowed the gap to thirty metres now and is mere seconds from hitting me. I find, though, that I have time to think, and plan. Three things cross my mind. Firstly, I am sorry that I am going to die this way. It's embarrassing. (Really, Lloyd? A croc? In a small boat? You should have known better). Secondly, and bizarrely, I don't want to get my treasured binoculars wet. They cost me a small fortune some years ago, and I really don't want them submerged. And finally, I know that crocs sometimes don't simply crash into their intended victim's boats but will occasionally surge high up out of the water and snatch people off them, leaving the craft upright. An old man in Botswana's Okavango Delta, a man called Zobra, taught me that.

So I lie down. At the very last second I lie down in the bottom of the boat, lowering its centre of gravity, and trust to fate. It is the only aspect of this self-inflicted disaster that I can actually control, and as the croc's bow wave splashes white only metres away, I flatten myself and hope.

The croc smashes *into* the canoe. Hard. The small craft rocks violently, and warm water cascades over me, pouring into the boat but miraculously it remains upright. Strangely, all fear flees from me now, and an unexpected aura of calm sets in. I grasp the paddle and begin to direct the boat towards the sand dune again. The original crisis had been the rapids, and I'm still drifting fast towards the rocks. Another surprisingly rational thought crosses my mind: paddle in long slow sweeps, make no white water, be controlled, show no sense of panic.

The crocodile is gone. I hope.

But this species survived the meteor impact of sixty-five million years ago: crocodiles have been around a long time precisely because they seldom miss a feeding opportunity. They're cunning. He might still be here somewhere. I hit the bank, and hurl myself onto the sand dune. I once witnessed a crocodile in the Kruger National Park propel itself metres up a steep bank and pull a struggling Nyala antelope into the water. That's in my mind as, horrifyingly, I slide back into the water, up to my waist. With desperate haste I scramble up the dune, sand flying from beneath my feet and hands, my binoculars (still dry) flailing about my neck and chest, and claw my way upwards to safety. I gain the top, screaming in the exultation of being alive, maniacally shouting to the bright black rocks and the cobalt sky.

And right there next to that little boat, that fragile bobbing little boat, the crocodile surfaces, water cascading off his back. I'm back in my own natural element, safe for now and on hard ground. I'm high and dry, but I'm trapped. Scattered about me lie small boulders of black basalt, fist-sized and plentiful. I direct a fusillade of rocks down upon the croc, hurled with all the venom and hate and accumulated fear I can muster. Five, then ten, ever-larger boulders strike that croc, and he never moves. He just floats there. He's insidious and patient – an awful, sinister combination.

The sun, at its mid-afternoon zenith, is now very hot, and I tire eventually of trying to exact retribution. I'm trapped and the croc seems to know it. There is no shade at all. Even so, risking getting back in that boat is not an option. Despite the heat, I am shivering as the panic subsides. I'm becoming dehydrated and feeling desolate, but it's better than the naked cold fear of being attacked on that remote African river. I'm not getting back in that canoe.

So I'm forced to play the waiting game, too. And hours later when the camp manager comes looking for me in the long aluminium outboard boat, and finds me on my sand dune, now parched and sun-reddened, that horrible old crocodile is still there, the bloody old flatdog, waiting. As the rescue boat arrives, he sinks slowly, very slowly away.

We tow that ridiculous canoe back to camp where I smash it up with a heavy mallet.

And I have never seen a Cinderella Waxbill to this day.

2

BLACK VELVET

Mamba! I can see straight down its throat!

It's a real headline grabber, this one. My boring game drive has just come to life in sudden and electrifying fashion.

Every guide has a Black Mamba story, often apocryphal, invariably exaggerated, always eagerly absorbed by story-hungry guests around the evening fire, their whisky forgotten and the ice melting, their mouths open in rapt attention. They shift uncomfortably and start looking under their chairs. Just in case. This is the snake that always dominates safari conversations. Everyone's heard of it. It's always featured on those type of television programmes called "Africa's Top Ten Most Deadly". It's the one that always causes a thrill to run down the spine. I had been guiding at Mala Mala a full year before I could stop telling other guides' mamba stories, because I found my own.

In "Slow Train Coming," Bob Dylan sings a song about naming all the animals.

"He saw an animal smooth as glass, slithering his way through the grass."

But Bob just can't bring himself to say the word "snake" in that song. A lot of people are like that. They won't give a snake a tag, as if by not acknowledging it the threat ceases to exist. When I tell people what I do for a living, they always ask me about snakes, and to be honest, it is the only kind of animal that freaks me out. Just a little. It's something to do with the shape of their heads. Sinister. Those beady little eyes. The flickering tongue. The silent fluidity of their progress into places they don't belong. It's crazy how a snake can even *move* without legs. Some guides like to handle snakes, to pick them up, put them down their shirts, to keep them as pets. Not me. Two of my guiding colleagues have been bitten by Puff Adders: one lost a finger and the other very nearly lost his life. The damn fools were being macho, showing off. I still have all my digits and I intend to keep them. Snakes have their place and I would never harm one, but when I see them, even the non-venomous types (which is most of them, actually), I prefer to watch them from a distance.

The Bible has a lot to answer for. The Book of Genesis didn't do snakes any favours. What if the prophet had said: "Oh, you know, those snakes, aren't they cool? God was in *great* form when he thought *them* up. Must have been a Monday animal. So friendly, so beautiful. And they're all neck, that's the great thing. Never trust an animal with a short neck, folks!" But no. He dissed them. And now they're forever stuck with a bad rap. So when a snake slides into view, everyone goes crazy, calling the police, the fire brigade, an ambulance, looking for rocks and sticks and other missiles, and leaping about on top of the furniture.

It's a late wintry morning at Mala Mala Game Reserve in the Mpumalanga Lowveld when my own mamba story begins. I'm rattling back to Kirkmans' Camp, the lodge where I'm based, in an ancient Land Rover 109 called "K2", a sly old beast of a car that can go anywhere but has a tendency to cough to a stop with loud belching noises after crossing deep rivers. It's been a quiet and bitterly cold game drive, the denizens of the bush hunkered down and hidden, and the German guests on the vehicle behind me are mute and downcast, wrapped in thin, grey blankets. They're first-timers on safari, classic victims of 'The Big Five syndrome', intent on ticking off only the long-toothed, the long-tusked or the long-horned species on their mammal lists. They are palpably unhappy; they've been with me for only two drives and I've already found them the big cats, elephants, buffalos ... but I haven't found them a rhino. They sit hunched and censorious, their faces pinched from cold and disappointment, and from their dark Teutonic muttering I discern that this, their final game drive, is not matching up to the promises that their travel agent made them.

"Vot time do ve see ze Reeno?" asks Heinrich.

They have a plane to catch at noon so I'm hurrying them back towards a hearty brunch, but I can imagine the discontent that will arise from delivering six grumpy Germans to camp even a moment before the stated time. I need to use up ten minutes, so not far from camp I turn along a little-used track, cross the old Selati railway line, and drive into an area of low *Acacia* scrubland. The bush is grey and dusty, the rank grass tall and ill-looking, untouched yet by the rib-flanked herds of buffalo that are struggling to find enough fodder to see them through the harsh, dry winter.

Immediately, I flush a Black-backed Jackal. It zigzags, unconcerned, around some spreading thicket and then accelerates away, seeing that I am following at a short distance. It's an anticlimax compared to the White Rhino we have been looking for all morning, but the drive has been devoid of excitement, so I stay on his tail.

There is something that happens on a game drive occasionally that widens a guide's eyes and causes his heart to lurch. It is when a front wheel strikes an old, dead stick lying concealed in the grass, just so. The stick leaps up, sometimes slamming hard and suddenly into the fender with a startling crack, shattering into pieces and spraying splinters and helpless termites into the air. Less often, but more seriously, it cartwheels up and into the vehicle, scaring the blood from guest's faces, even causing it to flow if it whips across a brow or a cheek. It is a great embarrassment to a guide, but it is usually borne with good humour, even sometimes enjoyed with hilarity, by the guests who don't mind seeing their otherwise unflappable khaki warrior discomfited and alarmed.

I swing the open-topped game drive vehicle around some scrub and find myself approaching an *Acacia* thorn cul-de-sac that forces me to slow down as the jackal slips away through a low gap in the bush. Without warning, a thick black stick leaps up beside me, right alongside the door-less driver's seat. Instead of falling back to earth, the stick stays there, upright, motionless.

Black Mamba! This is no stick! It's an angry mamba, and it is thirty centimetres from my face.

My heart stops, everything slows right down, and I freeze.

We've come across it so fast that it has had no time to slither away. It has risen in sudden, agitated self-defence, and is facing me at head height. We're eye to eye. A hundred thoughts race through my mind, among which the phrase "certain death" features prominently. I sit immobile and helpless, and in that peculiar moment when time seems to have stopped I notice in an oddly detached way some minute details: the parallel patterning of its breast scales and the way the morning sun is glinting in its obsidian eyes. It opens its mouth and expels a shockingly loud gust of air, its neck swelling and flaring a little. Staring transfixed into its broad-gaped maw, I see only blackness. Like velvet, all light is absorbed by that soft, dark, deep interior. The fangs, surprisingly small, are yellow-white and menacing. Quite undisturbed by this drama, a Cape Turtle Dove calls quietly nearby.

Still the black snake rears there, immobile, rigid. There's no sound from the horrified Germans behind me. Then panic asserts itself, and my left boot slips with a bang off the clutch. The Land Rover hurtles forward as it stalls, burying its nose into the *Acacia*, bringing the mamba abreast of the *fraulein* sitting directly behind me. She begins to keen, a low moan of terror, a wail in anticipation of impending doom. But this turn of events now, and at last, is too much for the unnerved snake. It suddenly drops in a writhing mass of sooty coils, raises itself up again, and "esses" away from the vehicle, its big head aloft and perfectly visible above the intervening scrub as it makes a rapid and welcome exit.

The keening stops. A long, shocked silence ensues. A small wind plays in the dried leaves around the car. The dove coos on. Despite the wintry chill, my khaki shirt sticks wetly to my back, and small drops of moisture stand out on the tops of my hands. I collect myself and turn to the guests to begin some feeble apology, but their expressions of horror, their white-knuckled grip on the seat-fronts, tell me that no words will be adequate.

"We go now, yes," says Heinrich, firmly.

"We go," I agree.

I re-start the Land Rover, reverse out of the thorn trap, and begin a slow and stunned drive directly back to camp. As we approach the boom gate, the Germans find their tongues, and begin to babble in awed excitement in the way that people do following a gripping experience. It is the noise of triumph shared by a group of friends who have faced Africa's most lethal serpent at point blank range, and escaped unharmed. Unexpectedly, they have become a Band of Brothers. There is nothing like a good story, especially if it is personal, particularly if it is true, and oh, what a story they now have to tell their Stuttgart friends.

Heinrich is elated. In a pleased tone that indicates that I have vindicated myself, that this game drive had become an unmitigated success, he enquires:

"You see many snake like zis one?"

"My first mamba," I say happily.

3

MOBILING

"Lloyd! Stop!"

His scream shatters the cold dense air, and now there are lions running everywhere, streaks of tawny, long-fanged cats pelting through the scrub. And it's not only the lions that are running. Mompati and I are hoofing it out of there at top speed too. I'm not sure I'm going to get away this time.

Sophie, an elegant journalist for a British women's magazine arrived yesterday at Zibalianja Camp. She sat sipping an evening gin and tonic at the bar under the Apple-leaf tree without even getting her lipstick wet. She's on a freebie with Linyanti Explorations, for whom Sue and I manage the camp, and our boss has sent a message through on the dodgy old High Frequency radio: we need a great piece out of this. Over to you.

"Lions," she's told me with winning emphasis. "Big male lions. I've seen everything." (*Everything*? Really?) "I've seen leopards mating and wild dogs hunting and elephants swimming, but so far no one has shown me big male lions. And this is my last camp before I fly back to England tomorrow. I've got one game drive left. I want lions."

So no pressure, then. But she's come to the right place. Here on Selinda Reserve we are currently blessed with a coalition of three brothers, big chaps about six or seven years old, coming into their full power and utterly dominant over all pretenders to their throne. More importantly, they are quite easy to find because they restrict their territory to the grassy floodplains between the *mopane* woodland and the Zibalianja Lagoon, patrolling for hippos that have to leave the sanctuary of the water at night to feed. Some nights we are woken by a terrible screaming in the reeds that fringe the lagoon, and then we know: the lions and their female consorts are on a hippo, and in the morning the circus will begin, a bloody three-day gathering of big cats, hyenas and patient vultures, each feeding in turn, while the blood and guts of their victim soaks into the grass. It's not a sight for the faint-hearted. If that happens, it will be interesting to see how our English writer bears up. A lion covered in gore emerging from within the body cavity of a stinking hippo doesn't match up to the Disney-esque view of the regal King of the Bush with flowing mane and majestic pose. A journalist for a fashionable magazine for "ladies who lunch" will find it difficult to include a piece describing how lions scavenge and eat rotten meat. It spoils the magic.

"There are three lions out there waiting for you, Sophie," I told her. "Three big boys."

I'm confident. Not from me the usual prevarications and cautions you hear from most guides. We can't guarantee anything out here in the bush, they say. There's no script, this is not Animal Planet, they tell guests. Nonsense: the three brothers are out there, we see them almost daily and best of all, I have a young trainee guide called Mompati, very eager to rise above his current role as waiter, who goes out with me every day to learn. He's good, Mompati, with sharp eyes and a fine understanding of what guests need. We'll find the lions.

The lions go by names. Grant over at Selinda Camp has called the dominant brother Rufus because of his rust-coloured mane. His more cowardly brother, the pale one with the scars on his backside (he's always running away from a fight), is called Blondie, of course.

The middle brother has gone without a moniker for a while, but I have started calling him Tog: The Other Guy. Blondie's reticence in conflict notwithstanding, they are a formidable group. I tell Sophie about them, calling them by name. Some guides are hesitant to give individual animals names, fearing that they somehow diminish the animals by anthropomorphising them, but I don't mind it. The guests do it anyway, creating fantasy conversations between the animals, expressing what they think the animals are thinking. It's a natural human reaction to name things and to personalise animals. Furthermore, when it comes to writing a mainstream magazine article, you need to characterise the animals; it's not a scientific journal, so calling an animal something like "ZS 62" doesn't wash. Nope, it's got to be Broken Ear or Stumpy. Or Rufus.

Sophie listened intently as I related tales of these hippo hunters. It's unusual behaviour that crops up in this area from time to time. Although there are plenty of other, smaller prey species about, Selinda lacks herds of buffalo, and when a large meal is required to feed a big pride of lions, smaller antelopes like Impalas won't suffice. Somehow, the lead female in the pride has learned to wrap herself around the jaws of a hippo, preventing it from using its fearsome weapons, long stabbing and cutting teeth, while the remainder of the pride swarm over the downed animal, tearing at its eyes and ears, biting into its neck, bearing it to ground by weight of numbers. It's usually at this time that the three boys arrive, lending their considerable bulk to the contest, and ripping into the hippo through the belly and anus, the easiest ports of entry into a thick-skinned animal. A hippo cannot be throat clamped and asphyxiated like most of the lions' victims: the neck is too fatty. So instead the poor animal gets eaten alive, dismembered, bellowing its life away, and eventually (mercifully) it dies when a major artery is ruptured.

They don't show that bit on Animal Planet. And it will find no place in Sophie's glossy magazine.

But tonight it is quiet in the African bush. I raise my head from my pillow from time to time to listen to the distant calling of lions, but they are far away and there is no answer from the Selinda boys.

A little flutter of anxiety rushes through me. Then, an hour before dawn, Rufus and his brothers come to life. Their roaring and counter-roaring rolls across the darkened grassland, reaching a crescendo that is the most thrilling sound in the African bush. I am fully awake in a second, tumbling into khaki clothing, dragging on thick socks and heavy boots, a beanie and gloves, a warm jacket. It is mid-June, and absolutely frigid outside. Sue murmurs something from the cosy confines of the bed, wishing me luck probably, but already I am zipping the tent closed and on my way. This is what I love.

The inestimable Mompati has already rejuvenated the fire and is stirring a considerable quantity of sugar into his coffee in the African way. As I fetch my rifle and bring the safari car around to the fireside, he pours me a big enamel mug-full from the kettle that is steaming and hissing on the coals.

"I have woken Sophie," he says. "The boys are near the Savuti Channel. But they are mobiling east."

This is Motswana guide-speak meaning that the lions are on the move. He is as excited as I am, grinning broadly in the flickering firelight, ready to get out there and track lions. This pre-dawn start is a little unusual, actually. Game viewing in winter can be slow in the frosty mornings: mammals like us usually prefer to wait for the sun to warm them a little before they get moving. But the brothers are out there and Sophie needs lions. Mompati gets it.

He's about to get a hell of a lot more. There's going to be plenty of mobiling this morning, mobiling of the fastest kind.

A flashlight beam comes wobbling down the path. Sophie emerges from behind it, bundled up like us, roused earlier than she had anticipated. I'm happy to see how eager she is, even in the cold and dark. Many safari guests find it difficult to get going in the morning, needing to drink a slow coffee and struggling with their equipment in unaccustomed darkness. It's maddening when the lions are calling, and the guests are showing no urgency. You can't press "pause" at a live show.

That's not the case today. Sophie gets it too. I thrust an insulated mug of English breakfast tea into her hands, and we're away, the rapier beams of our headlights slicing through the blackness. An amazed Redbilled Francolin bursts from a low roadside *Acacia* shrub, chattering its displeasure. We're on the hunt.

It is very, very cold in the open vehicle and the air feels thick. Sophie is mute in the back, snatching a sip of tea when the lurching of the Land Cruiser allows it. I stop every ten minutes or so to listen, but the roaring has stopped: what does this mean? It may simply be that Rufus feels that he and his band have yelled enough to warn off any potential competitors. Job done. In fact, lions have an annoying habit of suddenly going quiet as the sun rises, but keeping on walking. As a guide, you have to anticipate their movement, plot their likely course based on where the noise was last heard, exploit your knowledge of their particular idiosyncrasies: where do they usually patrol, where do they like to lie up, where do they prefer to drink? It's not an exact science and that's where tracking comes in: cutting the fresh *spoor*, leapfrogging it, casting ahead, using some educated guesswork and working it all out. It's a fun game, and extremely rewarding when you get it right. The clients love it and often try to get involved, pointing out tracks – sometimes days old – and the anticipation grows, so when you finally round a corner and point out your quarry, everyone is amazed and triumphant.

We find the tracks quickly. They're so fresh that the lions have barely stepped out of them. They are heading directly towards the nearby Savuti Channel that marks the border of the concession. We are not allowed to cross it, but the lions can. Mompati glances at me. "Let's move it," he's saying, "once they've crossed, no more lions for us." No more lions means grumpy Sophie. And the tepid magazine article she will write won't please our boss. More importantly, we want to finish what we have started here. We're on a mission.

Rufus and company have passed this way all right and, even better, they are accompanied by the entire pride, perhaps four adult females and their cubs of various ages. Including the heavy artillery, that's about twelve lions. The tracks go straight into a thick clump of Bluebush, a dense thicket impenetrable to a vehicle, so I skirt around it, gunning the car, anticipating that the tracks will emerge from it on the other side, the Channel side. There's nothing.

We're confused. Mompati and I know these lions and we know what they usually do. And we're under time pressure to find them. No tracks emerge from the island of bush into which they have so recently walked. Perhaps we have been too hasty: I don't know how, but we must simply have missed them. I drive back around to the entry point and stop the Cruiser.

"Sophie," I inform our passenger as I exit the car, "Mompati and I will quickly follow the tracks through this patch of bush and find where they emerge on the other side, then we'll come back here and continue in the vehicle. Won't be long. They're not far."

Mompati and I start to walk swiftly down an elephant path through the thick stuff. I don't have my rifle with me, thinking we'll only be on foot for a minute or two. The lion tracks are everywhere, spread out over several broad elephant paths, and Mompati and I follow two parallel sets. We're numbed by the cold, but we're moving fast because the signs are clear and the pride is on the move.

A bird whistles, close to me, making some kind of alarm call. In some part of my pre-occupied brain, I register the call as being odd, not a call I know, but I am intent on the *spoor* and I keep walking, eyes down, focused on my task. A second later it whistles again, much louder this time, and urgent. The tracks are clean and bright. I ignore the call.

"Lloyd! Stop!" Mompati's warning comes, shockingly sudden and loud.

I look up instantly and in that split-second I know what I am going to see. There are lions everywhere. In front of me, not five metres away, sprawled across the pathway, limp and languid, piled upon each other in the numbing cold, lies the entire pride, briefly resting, a jumble of lions trying to stay warm.

But Mompati's scream, the scream that has saved me, has startled them into frenzied action. In a moment and with surprised gruff barks, they are on their paws, ears flat against their heads, tails lashing, making that belly growl that horrifies even the bravest of men. They are killing machines, galvanised by the sudden threat, ready for action, terrifying. And there are so many of them.

And then the moment is too much for any of us, lions and men, and we scatter: we all simply start to run. We "mobile" like crazy! It's perfectly pointless, I'm never going to get away, but there is nothing else to do, and this is no time for rational thinking. Instinct takes over. There's a pointy termite hill at hand and I sprint up it and spin around, waiting to be flattened by 250 kilograms of very angry lion. I can hear Mompati, the thunder of his big size-twelves, hammering away down the path towards the car. He's done what he can for me, it's save yourself now, and never mind the women and children.

But there's not a lion in sight.

I have no idea where they are, but I follow Mompati's example and go crashing again through the Bluebush towards the Cruiser, my breath loud and fierce and ragged, great plumes of it coughing from me like I'm an ancient locomotive. I reach the car just in time to see the bottom of Mompati's boots disappearing over the edge of the car door. He hasn't bothered to open it; he's just dived straight in. I follow.

We untangle ourselves and sit there, chests heaving, staring at each other, speechless. Sophie is wide-eyed but also amused. She's seen the lions, big and small, bursting out in every direction, and she is delighted. When I look around me, I find that the entire pride is scattered about at a distance on the damp Kalahari sand, in full view, staring suspiciously at the car. The pride is ruffled and confused but already beginning to relax.

Sophie leans forward. I notice now that she even had time to apply her lipstick this morning, and it's still perfect.

"Find them, then, did you boys?" she asks, laughing.

4

BEDSIDE MANNER

"Trust me, I'm a doctor."

It is extraordinary what power those words can hold for some. Take Erika, for example. Andre never even said it but Erika simply trusted. It was akin to a miracle.

"*Ipsala!*" she always liked to say.

I don't know what that means in Swiss German, or even how to spell it. Maybe it's just her own little expression, but she keeps repeating it and it's a good sign: it means that Erika is back. She's wolfing down a bowl of warm butternut soup with crusty, camp-baked bread, and sitting tall and upright in the lounge. It's good because she's been missing for twenty-four hours, zipped into the close confines of her dark safari tent at Zibalianja camp, zipped in with the oppressive heat and the black dust and the flies. And now I know why.

Erika is a pharmacist from Berne. She is tall, angular, clumsy, prone to knocking over glasses of wine and gesticulating lavishly with the cutlery as she tells stories at the dining table. She's also great fun, very quirky, highly-strung and wonderfully enthusiastic; the kind of guest that you remember fondly. This is her second safari with Sue and me at Zib. She was here in August last year and we all got on famously so I was pleased to see her name on the booking sheet again. At the airstrip yesterday Mompati and I laughed from beneath the "Domestic Arrivals Terminal", actually just a dark-leafed Sausage tree, at the spectacle of Erika struggling from the narrow confines of the Cessna 206, rake-thin and gangly, all tangled arms and legs and luggage, not even waiting for the prop-wash dust to settle to come dashing over to us. Erika's exuberance is legendary: she's prone to suddenly shouting out in the middle of sightings, causing sleeping lions to lift their heads in fright and galvanising their cubs into rapid retreat behind them for protection. With Erika, unpredictability comes with the territory, but I'll take that over blandness any day. Which is why what happened later was so mystifying.

"Oh, she'd said in a rush. How are you both? These little planes are so bumpy. And small. How old is that pilot, she looks nineteen!"

"She *is* nineteen," I'd replied. "Welcome back to Zib, Erika! How was the rest of your trip from Switzerland?"

"*Gut, gut,* okay. But the Swissair plane slid off the runway in Johannesburg this morning. It was raining and we didn't stop in time, I don't know what happened. It was quite scary but no one was hurt so it was all okay."

She'd seemed fine, though perhaps a little more fidgety and animated than I remembered. I put it down to the excitement of being back in the bush; the African wilderness always has an energising effect on people. I drove her slowly back to camp, steering across the grassy plain for the lovely Rain tree and the pair of Fan Palms that pinpointed our little island lodge, while Erika and Mompati chatted about what the lions were up to and when they had last killed. Dinner that night was infused with buoyant tales of the wild and Erika retired to her tent in good humour after a few glasses of South African Merlot, eager to get going early for her first game drive.

This morning I awoke to a hot, dry, suffocating wind which was bringing the dust of the desiccated plains with it, blowing a veil of grime into every gap and nook and cranny. Even the White-browed

Robins were cowed into submission, too intimidated to lead the morning bird chorus. Mompati had done the wake-up calls but had failed to elicit the usual enthusiastic answer from Erika.

"It is too quiet in there," he'd said, looking worried.

Odd. She's normally the first guest at the morning fire. I gave Erika a few minutes to emerge and then went to her tent to call her again. The other guests in camp were growing impatient, keen to get going before the arrival of first light.

"Erika?" I'd called loudly.

A weak, faltering voice. Uncharacteristic. But a response, at least.

"No game drive today. I must rest. I am okay. I have drugs."

"You sure? Okay, take it easy and I'll come and I'll see you when I get back from the drive. So you don't need anything?" I asked.

Very strange. She was all fired up last night, ready for adventure, full of brio, anxious to meet up again with Rufus, Tog and Blondie. She'd said that she'd been working very long hours leading up to the trip, trying to meet deadlines before departure: I guess it has all caught up with her, that's all. I'd seen this type of exhaustion set in before with guests who lead stressed lives and then find themselves abruptly in a place of peace: their mind and body lets go, demanding recompense. Plus, the heat and wind can make things unpleasant and have a peculiar effect on people's moods: it can be very unsettling when the tent flaps crack and whip in the breeze and dust devils whirl though the camp, flinging dry twigs and leaves against the canvas walls. Okay, I'd thought, let her recover, I'll track down those lions this afternoon to make up for it. She'll be all right.

I'd asked Sue to check on her periodically and guided the other guests on the activity, but when we returned for brunch, there was still no sign of Erika. Sue said she'd rejected the offer of a breakfast on her tent veranda, turned down coffee, which she normally drinks with relish, and had chased away the astonished laundry staff when they came to make the bed and freshen up the room. It's mid-afternoon now, almost time for another drive, the other guests will soon become restless, and she's failed to appear for tea. I need to get to the bottom of this. Something isn't right.

"Erika? Erika, I'm coming in. I have cold water and fruit for you," I call out as I approach her tent.

"No, no, keep the tent closed. Keep it closed! I'm not hungry." There's something urgent and afraid in her voice that further heightens my concern. She's hiding away from the world. I need to get in there immediately. I quickly invent a reason to come in.

"I need to check the pipes in your shower. There's a leak outside and the water is running all over the place. I won't be a minute," I say.

I gingerly open the door zipper, afraid of what I might find. It's like an oven in the tent, and it smells stale and lived-in. In the shadowy light I see that the fine black dust has crept in everywhere despite the closed door and window flaps, coating the surface of the table and the chairs, collecting along the tops of the picture frames. Erika is lying dishevelled on the bed, the sheets twisted and the pillows crumpled, her thin hair plastered to her sweaty forehead. Her suitcase is barely unpacked but on the spare bed is spread a kaleidoscope of drugs: capsules and tablets of many colours, potions and lotions, powders and pills of every kind. The waste paper bin is next to her bed and she has clearly been vomiting. Erika looks at me with child-like apprehension. She obviously needs immediate help.

"Erika, I'm going to move you, okay?" I say gently. "To the spare tent. You'll be much more comfortable there. Here, let me help you."

There's no point in asking her what's wrong. I doubt she even really knows herself. She is clearly frightened. She's been dosing herself with a cocktail of medicines, and she is woozy, embarrassed and bewildered. I scoop her up and she doesn't resist: she's probably dehydrated, and is as light as a sparrow. Sue and the staff move in and in short order we have her ensconced in a fresh new tent, all her goods and chattels moved along with her. A housekeeper has unceremoniously scraped up the assortment of drugs into a pillowcase, carried it over to the new tent and dumped it on the bedside table. Erika's eyes follow me as I sort through her medicines. Many of the bottles have been opened: they promise relief from nausea, pain, diarrhoea, and insomnia. A pill for every ill, it seems. I think she is afraid I will confiscate them.

"Erika, the lions are missing you. *We* are missing you. Do you think you can make it this afternoon?" I say, trying to encourage her.

"I am tired from the flight, that's all. But maybe I need a doctor. Can you get a doctor?"

Zib is several hours flight from the nearest medical doctor in Kasane or Maun, the closest urban settlements. It's possible, at great expense, to arrange to have a doctor flown out, and we'd do it in a life-or-death emergency, but Erika's situation is not that urgent. This calls for a more imaginative plan. Something local.

"A doctor? No. But let me see what I can do," I say with perfect confidence. "You just lie back and drink water and chat to Sue. No more drugs, okay! We'll take care of you."

Immediately I see hope flare in her eyes and the faintest flicker of a smile. Recovery has already begun. She's chosen not to be alone anymore, and that's a great start.

"Mompati," I tell him, "you'll need to take the rest of the folks on their drive today, please. I'm going to try to get Erika back on her feet."

I radio the Reserve HQ and explain the situation to Andre, the Selinda Reserve manager, telling him the story about the bad landing. He's an old bush guy: he's seen it all and this is exactly the kind of challenge he relishes. He loves to make a plan, and his solutions are usually inventive and unexpected. A brightness underlies his voice as it crackles through on the radio. I can visualise him beaming. Help (in some form) is on the way.

"Hang on, I'll be there soon," he says.

Sue and I wait with Erika. She's weakly sipping water and some of her colour has already returned. The buffeting wind has abated somewhat, and with the slow fading of the sun the air is cooling down a little: nature is starting to feel less threatening. Within half an hour we detect the sound of an approaching Land Cruiser and I go out to the car park to meet Andre. To my amazement he exits the vehicle dressed in a white lab coat and neat trousers, polished boots and wearing a genuine medical stethoscope around his neck. He looks like he's stepped straight off the set of some type of Bush Doctor sit-com. My mouth is hanging open and he laughs in that gravelly way of his.

"Doctor Andre is in the house," he says, grinning while plugging the scope into his ears. "You never know when these things will come in useful. Now, where is my patient?"

Bemused but impressed, I lead the way up the steps of Erika's new tent and push the flaps aside. Sue's face is a picture of disbelief but she disguises it well and makes way for Andre. Avoiding the chair, he sits beside Erika on the bed.

"Hello my dear," he says in a soothing voice, speaking a mixture of English and basic German. "I am Andre. Now, tell me, what is wrong?"

The advent of "Doctor" Andre! His dramatic appearance is so magical that it doesn't even occur to Erika to wonder from where this help has so quickly materialised. Andre takes her hand and measures her pulse, uses the stethoscope on her chest and back – "breathe in my dear, breathe out, good, very good" – then gently wipes the moisture from her brow with a cool washcloth, asking questions about how she has slept (very little), her eating (too nauseous), even her recent bowel movements. All the while he strokes her hand, making small noises of empathy – "Aah, I see, hmm, really?, good, good" – while he nods and smiles.

"In this dreadful heat and wind, we see this a lot out here," he says to her. "And you have travelled from the cold of Switzerland, haven't you? Travel can place a severe burden on the body, you know. You must remember to drink water, it's imperative. And what are these?" he asks, indicating the impressive drug collection in the pillow case.

Perching his spectacles on the end of his nose, he examines the various bottles and blister-packs carefully, noting which of them has been opened, and commenting:

"Yes, yes, this is excellent, I think. Aah yes, is this a good product? I see you have taken several of these. Hmm, yes, these also look like the right thing."

Erika is visibly relieved at this endorsement of her self-medication regime and is now sitting taller in the bed, looking much more alert and aware.

"Now, my dear, if you would just blow into this paper bag," requests Andre. "An old trick, I'm sure you know it. Excellent.

Deep breaths, please. Inhale and blow out. Again. Again. Good. Thank you. How do you feel?"

Erika's limp hand is still in Andre's. He pats it and lays it gently on the bed.

"I think I feel a bit better thank you, Andre," she smiles at him. "Am I okay?"

"*Jawohl*, Erika my dear, right as rain, I think you just need fresh air and some food and a little walk. I want you to come down to the lounge area with us – we'll help you, don't worry – but first a nice hot shower, a change of clothes and then in the lounge some of Sue's wonderful soup. At bedtime I suggest that you take two of these blue tablets and just one of these green ones, nothing else. Plenty of water and herbal tea. By tomorrow you will be right as rain, I promise you," he reassures her.

"Thank you Andre. You are right, this heat is terrible. And the wind! It drives you crazy. I don't know what happened to me. I will be fine now."

We troop out of the tent and leave Erika to shower and change. On the way down to the lounge area, Andre gives Sue and me a broad wink.

"Panic attack, nothing more," he says. "Probably just delayed shock. I think the plane going off the runway scared the hell out of her, much more than she realised, and then the small Cessna bucking up and down compounded it. I've seen it before. Fear is a strange animal. But confidence trumps it every time."

He twirls his stethoscope above his head in a small victory salute, jumps into his Cruiser and speeds away, scaring an indignant mongoose from the road verge. To everyone's immense relief, an hour later, in the sudden stillness of a perfect bush evening, Erika is in the lounge, spooning butternut soup with gusto. She's back.

"*Ipsala!* That Andre is very good, no? Like a doctor. And this soup is very tasty, Sue. After this, just a little of that marvellous red wine. Lloyd, tomorrow morning we go and find those boys, those three lions. They are missing me!"

5

TRANSFORMED

Alice is gaping at the lions, transfixed, and in the dim light spilling from the car dashboard I can see that she is crying. A deep primal force has entered her in this moment, and it will never leave. It is tangible magic; it is thrilling, rare, and welcome. These are tears of joy, speaking of something fulfilled. She is dabbing at her eyes with a little white handkerchief.

"Thank you young man. Thank you ever so much," she says to me.

She's eighty-five and has a wonderful sense of the ridiculous. She speaks like an actress in some BBC period piece, which I find quaint and endearing, and her spirit and enthusiasm makes it easy for me to go several extra miles for her. Alice has plunged headlong into Africa. She's woven guinea fowl feathers into her hair, there are copper bangles about her skinny wrists, she's even quoting from Hemingway's *"Green Hills of Africa"*. Before she came out to the Botswana wilderness she read the journals of Victorian explorers such as Livingstone and Speke: now she's here to see Africa for herself, and there is not a moment to lose.

Although Alice is virtually deaf and fairly immobile, she is undaunted. She has all the artificial assistance that modern medicine can provide: hearing aids, stainless steel hips, blood pressure pills, a new knee. But I've guided folk with these challenges before, and I really admire her indomitable British verve, so we'll manage fine. She's with us at Zibalianja camp in northern Botswana ("Bogswana: it's damp here, isn't it?" she laughs) for a full week, which is wonderful: we can have a *proper* African adventure in a week. Alice is delightfully and idiosyncratically posh, and was married for years to some type of Irish aristocrat: a baronet, I think. He's dead now and Alice seems to be spending the remainder of her years on travel and champagne. And fulfilling her life's dreams. Why not?

"Sue," she says impishly to my wife at dinner, "this is already my third night and I *still* haven't heard any lions roaring. Your husband says they clamour all night long, but I think he's making it up. The ones he's shown me just seem to lie around with their paws in the air, the lazy brutes. I really, *really* want to hear a lion roar! And not like that silly MGM one either!"

Our local trio of lions, Rufus, Tog and Blondie, have been declaiming to the starlit heavens for hours every night lately, often quite close to camp, but Alice doesn't have a chance of hearing them, even when she's awake. But then, as Billy the waiter brings the dessert through, the triumvirate sound off, not a kilometre distant.

"Shss, shss, listen, *listen*, Alice, they're roaring now, can you hear them?" I say urgently.

But Alice is chatting loudly again with Sue, semi-shouting as deaf people do, and she can't hear me. I thump my spoon on the table and they look up at me, startled.

"Into the car. Now! Mompati, bring the Cruiser, chop chop! Billy, lend Alice a hand. Quickly!"

The old girl is up immediately, grabbing her walking cane, leaning on Billy, limping towards the game drive vehicle. Dessert lies abandoned upon the table.

"Won't be long, Suze," I shout.

Sue is accustomed to this. She gives me a long-suffering look that says "sure, I've heard *that* before. These guides, they're the bane of the kitchen staff's lives, they're either late for meals or they go dashing off in the middle of them," but she's only pretending to be cross.

We head straight out onto the dried-out floodplain, jolting slowly through the deep imprints of elephant and hippo feet that lurk under the wilted grass. A Bronze-winged Courser, a night bird, scuttles away from the wheels with surprised, bright eyes, then whirrs off into the darkness. Alice is hanging on gamely, her liver-spotted hands gripping the roll bar tightly. Mompati is scanning ahead of us with the million-candle power spotlight, digging the beam into the shadows. There! The three cats are right ahead of us, now lying mute, watching our approach with indifference. Mompati knows his stuff. He immediately switches the light off so that he won't blind them, but also because he has a sense of drama; he knows that Alice and Billy haven't seen them yet. I can still just make out the shapes of the three boys in the faint starlight and I carefully pull up to within ten metres of them and kill the engine. We sit in silence for a while, listening.

"Where *are* these blessed lions, young man?" asks Alice after a while.

"Not too sure, Alice. Very close I think. When they roar, we'll know. Let's just listen," I reply.

I nudge Mompati and he flashes a smile: this is going to be fun. One of the lions suddenly flops noisily over in the flattened grass, the wind shifts, and the distinctive pungent smell of lions wafts into the car. The King of the Beasts can be a stinky old regent sometimes. Billy, lounging across the back seats, sniffs audibly, sits bolt upright, then slides with alacrity to the far side of the seat, shouting "hey, hey!", pointing at the lions. In the dark Alice completely misses this drama and Mompati admonishes Billy, holding a finger to his lips, telling him in Setswana to calm down and sit still. Billy complies, but he's not enjoying this game very much, and has wedged himself as far back as he can, whispering "yo, yo, yo" softly to himself and wishing he was back in camp. These crazy guides! Furthermore, he is thinking, the hot ginger pudding back at camp is getting cold. What a waste.

We sit and enjoy the natural blackness. Then Rufus starts to moan softly, the prelude to a full roar, and immediately his brothers take the cue, joining in. In seconds they are all at it, going hammer and tongs, each one at his own pitch and pace, their voices overlapping, flooding through and past us, rattling the car and physically agitating our internal organs, reverberating across the plains. It is an overwhelming sound, awesome in its power. It exemplifies everything that is magnificent about Africa.

Alice's face is active with emotion. The sound is so enveloping that she can't work out where it is coming from, and she is squinting in every direction, scouring the darkness. She's heard them this time all right. Mompati flicks the spotlight onto the grass just in front of the lions and the reflected glow betrays their whereabouts. Alice exclaims, her hands flying to her mouth.

"Oh! Goodness me. They're here! They're right *here*!"

The lions are on their feet now, their great maned heads thrust out before them, necks extended, legs braced against the might of the effort, challenging all comers, every part of each of them concentrated on this moment. It is staggering and humbling to be party to this display. They reach a full-throated crescendo and then begin to bring the call back to earth in a series of gasping coughs, each a little quieter than the last, until eventually they slump exhausted back onto their bellies.

Mompati chuckles and gives me a delighted thumbs-up. Billy looks cowed and overwhelmed. Alice's aged face is transformed – she looks young again. I watch her in the secondary glow of the spotlight as she mops at her eyes. A dream has been fulfilled.

"Thank you young man. Thank you ever so much," she says quietly.

6

OLD NELSON

Old Nelson has chosen to be kind. We are at his mercy and he has elected to let us off the hook. Good, because I've run out of moves. That was about to become extremely embarrassing. Possibly even fatal.

"This is very lovely, getting about like this on these enormous vehicles, but it must be quite different engaging the wildlife on foot," Alice had said to me as the day began, balancing an ancient pair of heavy black binoculars, which she calls her "Rommels", on the dashboard.

"Engaging." How perfectly expressed! I respect this elderly, charming client all the more.

"Very true, Alice," I reply. "Seeing the wildlife from the car can feel a bit detached, sort of like watching a movie. It's fantastic, of course, but actually being on *foot* with them does add a certain extra edge. It's the difference between watching the movie and reading the book. It's in the details."

"Mind you, young man, I'm very glad we weren't on foot with those three lions last night," she adds. "Still, it would be jolly nice to get some dust on these old boots."

There's a wistful yearning in her voice, an old echo from within that seems to be saying, "I've left this too late."

Not necessarily, I think to myself. I have something wonderful planned for Alice today. She can't get about too quickly and the usual bush walk is not an option. I'll need to be careful. But there are ways ...

I head the Land Cruiser north up the transit route along the *mopane* tree line. It's late winter, which means that there is no water lying in the backcountry. The shallow clay pans that filled up during the rains have dried up entirely now and the animals all need to come down to permanent water to slake their thirst. They'll come to the Zibalianja Lagoon, and Old Nelson is due. He's an ancient elephant, a gentleman of the bush, calm and dignified, and wonderful to behold as he makes his stately way down to the water. There he drinks and bathes in the blue coolness before retreating slowly to the shade and sanctuary of the *mopane* woodland for the next few days. He's set in his ways, always following the same broad path to the lagoon's edge. He's just what I need today for Alice.

We grind slowly in low-range gear through the thick Kalahari sand, scanning ahead, scaring up a little red Steenbok, a dwarf antelope, from its shaded day bed. Then, there he is! A considerate approach is required: Old Nelson is blind in his right eye and he doesn't like to be surprised. Furthermore, he is missing his left tusk, broken off years ago, the legacy of using it as a tool, or perhaps from youthful clashes with other bulls. He is named, of course, for Horatio, the victor of Trafalgar, and in these parts he has won many great battles of his own. But he's in his twilight years now: all he wants is quiet and solitude. As he hears the low whine of the transmission, he stops and contemplates us.

Alice and Old Nelson, two old-timers, commune with one another for ten minutes, exchanging thoughts. He looms over us, wrinkled and worn, still massive and powerful yet entirely without malice, and when he starts to move again towards the water, I defer, back-off and drive away to where I know he will soon be drinking. Alice's eyes are gleaming.

"That was wonderful, young man. So close! The things he must have seen in his life," she says thoughtfully.

We reach the lagoon and I conceal the car behind a clump of Feverberry *Croton*, a dense growth of leafy green shrubs that provides deep shade and perfect cover. Old Nelson's habitual path runs before us, about fifty metres away, and the view from within our foliage cave is excellent. The water stretches out past a raft of hippos to the reeds on the far side of the lagoon, and all about is open grassland, rendered short and manicured like a bowling green through persistent grazing. We'll see Old Nelson (and anything else) approaching from miles out.

"Right, Alice, out please," I instruct. "All you will need are your Rommels."

She's immediately delighted and intrigued.

"Here? But ... now then, what tricks are you up to?" she says, enchanted by the promise of adventure.

I place two deck chairs in the shade close to the edge of the *Croton* cave. We're completely hidden from view. Even the Red Lechwes grazing down at the bowling green don't know we are here.

"Now Alice, you'll need to trust me," I reply. "You'll see. You're going to love this. I want you to sit quietly. Absolutely no noise at all, not even whispering. We can point at things but no talking. Relax. I will show you what to do."

She nods her understanding and says nothing more. I bring my rifle from the car, and a bottle of mineral water for each of us. I show her that there are five rounds in the magazine, big .375 hard-nosed cartridges that can stop any large animal if well aimed, and explain that this is just a precaution. I lean the weapon against the bole of the tree. We're ready. Alice is apprehensive but calm, moving carefully in her seat, the old binoculars a heavy weight about her neck. Every so often she glances at me for reassurance and I smile back. Down at the water a Grey Heron, immobile and patient, scrutinises the shallows for fingerlings, while Whistling Ducks gather in safe little clusters nearby. A few Impalas troop down, quite unaware of us, dipping their muzzles into the silver water, starting back every now and then at some imagined threat, then re-gathering and drinking again. High, high above in the overarching blue sky a double vapour trail betrays the presence of a jetliner at 10,000 metres, heading south for Johannesburg, a long way ahead of its own noise.

The star of the show appears right on cue, swaying steadily down his path towards us. Old Nelson looks absolutely massive from ground level. Alice spots him, gasps, grabs my arm, and points excitedly. It appears at first that he is going to walk straight towards us, but I indicate the path in front of us to Alice and motion her to be calm. What a trooper she is: she sits back and brings her heavy binoculars to bear.

The elephant strolls steadily to water, scattering the Impalas with a lazy swing of his trunk and emits a deep belly rumble of anticipation. He's no more than fifty metres away from us. Nelson clears the water surface with the tip of his trunk, reaches in deeper and siphons in a column of cool, clean liquid that he tips into his mouth. We can hear it echoing down into his stomach like a waterfall. It sounds hollow in there: he's been away for three days and he's filling up. At his own deliberate pace Old Nelson drinks trunkfull after trunkfull, stopping every now and then to just stand and reflect. He has all the time in the world.

Alice is captivated. I know she wants to articulate what she is experiencing, but she remains quiet, her excitement betrayed only by the quite squeaking of the springs of the deck chair as she adjusts her position.

His thirst slaked, Old Nelson begins to cool off. He sprays water across his gnarly old hide, between the legs, on the belly, behind his great tattered ears, tossing water onto his back with practiced precision, turning himself a shining dark grey in the process. At last it is time for him to return to the *mopane* forest and Old Nelson turns to leave. To my immense surprise, the old fellow walks directly towards our hiding place. Alice looks at me fearfully. I motion for her to stay very still as I pick up my rifle. There is not even time to draw back the bolt and ram a round into the breech: Old Nelson, huge and unsuspecting, is already upon us. Not three metres away, he lazily begins to pluck Feverberry leaves, stripping them in clusters from the branches.

Our cover is being eaten from over us. Alice is leaning so far back in her chair that she is almost tipping over, but she's remaining composed. This remarkable woman even manages to give me a shaky thumbs-up.

My immediate concern is what might happen if, or rather when, Nelson suddenly detects us. The likelihood is that he will spin around and retreat, trumpeting in bewilderment, but what if he doesn't? What if he lurches forward to investigate, trampling us in the process? I need to let him know that we are here. But if I clap my hands now it would certainly alarm him: that would be way too threatening. Instead, I slowly reach to my belt and pull out a spare .375 round. I hold it up to Alice. She looks horrified. "No, no," I indicate, shaking my head, "don't worry, I'm not going to shoot him!"

Old Nelson towers over us, still insensible to our presence, happily feeding. I tap the brass bullet casing very, very quietly on the barrel. Old Nelson takes a short step closer. His trunk is now right above us, reaching deeper into the *Croton*. Alice shrinks even lower in her chair. This is getting pretty scary now. I tap again, louder. He's making so much noise defoliating the shrubs that he can't even hear me. Three times I tap, each time louder, and on the third noise the giant bull suddenly stops dead. He freezes. So do Alice and I.

Nelson raises his head a little, and listens. I tap the cartridge firmly again. In the stillness it sounds like the chiming of a tiny pocket watch. He stands motionless, his trunk still poised above our heads. We are trapped. Old Nelson needs to make the next move. For several excruciatingly long seconds the giant old elephant stands there, and then he begins to reverse slowly out of the thicket. I sense that he's thinking: "what's in there? What did I just hear? Whatever that was, it didn't quite belong. There are other things to feed on, anyway. Time to leave." Nelson strolls back down to his path, stops to cast a final suspicious look in our direction, then begins his slow return walk to the *mopane*.

It feels like I haven't breathed for minutes. Alice is absolutely delighted. What an experience, what a story she has to tell. Africa has spoken, and settled in her soul again.

"So how do you like engaging wildlife on foot, Alice?" I ask her quietly.

"Young man," she says breathlessly. "Last night the lions and now this! That was extremely invigorating! With the exception of the night that I met my husband, this safari has been the single most thrilling experience of my life. Thank you!"

7

SCREAMING BANSHEE

I crank the ignition key. Nothing happens. I try again. The starter motor makes a discouraging clicking noise. In desperation, I turn the key once more and incredibly the Land Cruiser fires up. I'm profoundly relieved, yet I'm gunning the car straight at her. The old Banshee and her acquiescent daughter want us dead. This is going to be bloody close.

What did we do to you, old lady? What precipitated this undeserved wrath? We were just quietly rolling down Kanawe's Road in the Selinda Game Reserve, winding through the pungent Turpentine grass that grows nearly a metre and a half high here, minding our own business, came around a corner and there you were, you and your offspring, standing with your backs to us on a termite mound, picking at the sweet fruits of a Woolly Caper bush. And I'd switched the car off. Because Ray said he'd *fixed* the problem with that starter.

"This morning we'll explore a bit," I'd said to Sylvia and Anne over our fireside coffee at Zibalianja Camp. "We'll head north to Twin Pools. It's quite a distance along the transit route so we'll take Kanawe's shortcut through the high grass."

Kanawe is a smokey-eyed guide over at Selinda Camp. I can only think that he must have been badly lost one night and had to force this route back to the main road to Kwando because it's a bit of a waste of time, really: beyond the odd Kudu or other antelope, I never seem to find any animals on it. But it is a useful diversion if you're coming from Zib via the hippo pools.

Sylvia and Anne are South African safari enthusiasts, very entertaining company and the kind of guests who frequently immerse themselves in the wilderness and savour the way that nature offers something new every day, around each new corner. While Anne is measured and quietly appreciative, Sylvia tends to be emotional and excitable, prone to fascinating flights of imagination. Today, it turns out, the Banshee will ensure that no amount of hyperbole is required.

My Land Cruiser is known on the Reserve as the Brothel Creeper. It's a diesel-powered machine, and diesels are usually quite noisy, but for some reason this one chugs along on game drive with very little engine din, so I can sneak about the Reserve without really disturbing the wildlife. However, it is also prone to unpredictable electrical dysfunction: sometimes, out of the blue it just won't start. Yet, when I take it to Ray, our mechanic, it starts first go, like when you make an appointment to see a doctor and then when you get there all your symptoms have magically (and annoyingly) disappeared. Yesterday I invited Ray to join us on a game drive to demonstrate the problem. I stopped to look at the Selinda Pride near Bee-eater Island, lions lazing all around the car, their tails flicking at the flies, and sure enough, when it was time to move on, the car wouldn't start. I gave Ray an "I told you so" look. It was too dangerous to disembark from the Cruiser with the felines so close by, so Ray crawled out over the hood, somehow gymnastically gained access to the engine compartment while the astonished lions eyed him with deep suspicion, rectified the problem simply by tweaking some plugs and wires, and away we went. Sylvia and Anne were very impressed. I was less surprised: these bush mechanics are incredible. Give them a screwdriver and a length of number eight wire and they can make a functional space rocket. But can Ray *keep* the

Brothel Creeper going? I'm not so sure.

"So there's no problem with the car now?" Sylvia had asked hopefully this morning as Mompati brought the Cruiser through the gloom to the front of camp, it's headlights throwing wild shadows into the darkness.

She's of nervous disposition, keen as mustard but somewhat timid. Anne is more phlegmatic, and a little amused by her friend's concern.

"Oh, Syl," she'd smiled ironically, "what could possibly go wrong?"

"Ray *says* she's fixed," I'd said. "He's changed the battery and tightened all the connections. Let's go: Africa awaits!"

Sylvia had looked sceptical as she climbed into the vehicle, and not without reason. That's what I told her yesterday, too. The Brothel Creeper may play up again and she knows it. Ray has cautioned me to always park high on a termite mound if I want to switch off the engine, so that I can run-start the car if necessary. I'll try to keep that in mind.

We'd briefly admired some hippos as they exhaled blasts of breath into the dry Kalahari air and then cruised north onto Kanawe's road, not expecting to find anything exciting at all; and suddenly here they are, a tuskless female elephant and her calf, feeding on the Caper bush.

Surprised, I brake immediately and instinctively switch off the car. That might have been a mistake, I think to myself. Well, never mind. The elephants at Selinda are generally very relaxed, perfectly used to vehicles, so it'll be fine.

Without hesitation, without warning, without any apparent provocation, and to my utter amazement, the mother elephant comes straight for us, a Banshee in full flight. There is no shrill trumpet, no shake of the ears, no half-lunge forward, no kick at the dust, none of the usual warning signs. Instead, she rushes at us in an immediate, eerily silent but full-blooded charge that leaves me confounded. I feel the blood drain from my face and the old familiar pounding in my ears. Sometimes it's snakes. Sometimes it's lions. Or crocs. Or sharks. Or mountains. This time it's an elephant. Here we go again!

"Namibian elephant!" screams Mompati, his face alive with anxiety. "Go!"

A Motswana is quick to blame all aggressive elephants in northern

Botswana for being ill-mannered Namibian interlopers. Up here on the nebulous frontier with Namibia, where the Kwando river spreads into the confusing papyrus swamp that divides the two countries, animals wander across the border with impunity. But not immunity. Any that roam east may be at risk. Not all of the Namibian side is protected national park: much of it is community-farming land where villagers scratch a living from the unwilling soil, growing maize and pumpkins and millet. In other words, easy and succulent food for elephants. There is an age-old conflict between the people and the elephants that occasionally escalates into violence, especially since the end of the South African occupation of Namibia. That conflict made weapons, especially AK-47 assault rifles, easy to get your hands on. When a herd of elephants has, in a single night, destroyed your crop, the fruit of your season's labours, your very livelihood, well then, understandable desperation combined with a few rounds of 7.62 mm ammunition can provide an easy revenge. Sometimes the elephants are killed, sometimes merely wounded, sometimes simply alarmed. Inevitably, the harassment makes many of them ill-tempered, jumpy and suspicious of every human they encounter forever afterwards. Especially if they have youngsters to protect.

We are only a few kilometres from the nearest Namibian village here. We have arrived suddenly and almost silently in the Brothel Creeper. We've instantly altered the balance of the Banshee's world. And so she is charging us.

"Go, go, go! Oh God!" screams Sylvia.

I know that elephants scare her; I've noticed her flinching away from even the most gentle of them. She didn't even like being too close in a game drive car to Old Nelson, that majestic yet benign elephant.

The Turpentine grass towers above my head, and I know that the terrain on each side of the road is pitted with Aardvark holes, rotting tree stumps, and soft, yielding sand. I certainly can't drive in there. And I definitely can't reverse the car at the speed I need to if I am going to dodge this old cow. There's only one option: go forward. Pronto. Furiously forward, straight towards mayhem.

If the car starts.

The Banshee has only fifty metres to cover and she has the advantage of a downhill start, plunging in a short curve off the termite mound on which she was just feeding, her unquestioning calf following closely at her heels. She'll be here in just a few seconds. If she punches into us at that speed (and all my experience tells me that she's not going to stop) she'll roll this game-viewer like a log. I need to get around her; it's our only chance.

The motor clicks, then starts. I power forward, gaining momentum. There's no time to explain and this tactic is the very last thing that Sylvia and Anne are expecting. As I reach second gear, Sylvia goes crazy. She's leaning over me from behind, cursing, flailing at my broad brimmed hat in fear.

"No, no, no! Go back. Go back. Go back!"

Her binoculars swing forward heavily and crunch into the back of my head, but I am only faintly aware of it. We're closing the gap fast now and I've surprised the old elephant. She has to turn a little, to adjust her aim, and that's slowing her down. Her calf is getting under her feet, the poor little animal confused and frightened, its trunk flailing wildly. The road ahead of us beckons like light at the end of a tunnel, clear and free. Mompati is hanging on grimly to the grip handle on the dashboard, a tight resigned grimace on his face. This is going to be *bloody* close.

The Banshee's shadow begins to loom, her mad mahogany eyes startlingly clear and close but we're beginning to win this race. If she does hit us, it'll be at the back seats where no-one is sitting. This is only a marginal improvement: she could still bowl us over and smash us up. Then at the last moment we burst clear and she powers past just behind us, missing by a metre, her momentum carrying her across the road and into the long grass. I keep going, the car bouncing wildly, tossing my passengers about like rag dolls, as I try to make some distance. This is not over. She's trumpeting now, the Banshee, screaming at us in a long, frustrated shriek, and with a high-pitched squeal the calf joins in.

Okay, good, situation handled, all safe: we have the weather gauge now and I start to slow the car down at a safe distance. My skull hurts where the binoculars have clobbered it. Mompati is laughing with delight. His hand reaches over and covers the ignition key. Do not switch the car off, he is indicating. Sylvia misinterprets this and panics.

"Hey! What are you doing? Don't do that! Let's go. Keep going!" she shouts.

Anne looks a bit shocked by all the excitement, but I think she's actually rather enjoying it all. Now that we are safe, that is. Mompati stands in his seat to look back down the road. His face changes and he makes a strangled noise.

"Lloyd, go. She's here!" he yells.

Cunning old cow. She's back on the road again and coming noiselessly and fast. There still seems to be unexacted revenge on her mind. She starts to scream at us again, a horrible, high agonised trumpeting that splits the air, and I gun the engine and drive right out of sight, around several bends, disappearing in the lanky grass. This is met with universal approval by all the people on board. The old lady needs a break. So does Sylvia. Mompati looks at me with raised eyebrows.

"Those Namibians," he says, shaking his head.

I'm not sure if he's referring to the elephant or the people with whom they struggle to co-exist.

8

ORANGE PEELS
IN THE FIRE

Topside doesn't like me. I don't know why but we've just never got on. And he likes me a whole lot less after what I've just done. None of it makes sense to me, but I can't fault the evidence I'm seeing before me.

Xigera Camp is a green and leafy paradise in the very heart of the Okavango Delta. The annual flood just keeps coming this year, creeping higher every day, sneaking down the pathways and into the tents, lapping over the wooden bridges, slowly infiltrating the guts of our isolated little camp. Willie, an old timer who has been transporting goods and constructing lodges around these floodplains for years, says that many of the safari camps will go under this year.

"These Johannesburg business people and their fancy architects fly here in their chartered planes and they tell us to build camps here, and build camps there. They never listen; they just talk about occupancy rates and triple bottom line and completion deadlines and I don't know what. But they pay, so we build. Look at the marks on this Jackalberry tree, man! You see? Look how high they are. Two metres, *boet!* Those are floodmarks from twenty years ago. Still here. I show them, but they don't want to see those marks, these bloody Johannesburgers. They only see tourist dollars. Your camp is going under too, my friend. Start filling sand bags."

This is not good news. The airstrip, our only lifeline to the outside world, is already getting soggy, and having a small river running through our tent makes Sue and me uneasy. There are very few guests who appreciate that having a small crocodile in semi-permanent residence on their tent verandah ought to be the experience of a lifetime, whatever they might boast once they get back home. There is no way that we can move the guests to a drier camp: it is May, all the lodges are full and we can't afford the lost revenue anyway. The toilet sumps are full of water, the roads are subsiding, the guests are getting grumpy. Sue and I are at our wits end. I radio the lodge owner in Maun.

"Make a plan," he tells me. "That's why you are called the manager. What do you need?"

I make a plan and I send a list of required materials. He sends in Craig, a carpenter/builder, and we start moving the tents to higher ground, closer to the middle of the island, re-installing electrical wiring, re-routing and pumping out water-logged plumbing, relocating solar panels and hefting the furniture, all while the guests are out on activities, watching elephants and hippos and looking for Fishing Owls. We're doing a lot of all-day boat trips with the guests now to keep them out of camp so that we can get the work done. Hell, even the "game drives" are water activities this flood season – we're driving the Land Rovers through one-metre-deep water down flooded roads for kilometres on end.

All of the guest mattresses have became a little bit damp in the move, and soon they develop a musty odour that becomes embarrassing. The logistics crew in the village of Maun, our headquarters and re-supply point, dispatch new mattresses in a large six-wheel-drive Henschel truck. The Henschel is a beast of a machine, usually able to ford very deep stretches of water under a heavy load, but the flood this year has got the better of even it, and one mid-afternoon a radio call comes through to camp from the driver, Topside.

"We cannot cross at the drift near the baobab," he informs me.

He sounds grumpy. As the heron flies, he's not too far from camp so Craig and I set off in a light aluminium boat, equipped with an under-powered outboard Evinrude, to recce the situation. There's no clear channel to follow and soon we find ourselves navigating to the drift by dead-reckoning, fouling the propeller on waterlilies, reeds and grass, sometimes pushing the boat through knee-deep water, and often poling the craft across the inundated grass plains. Things are not going according to plan.

A baobab tree towers over the southern horizon, which tells us that we are approaching the drift. We eventually reach the vehicle where Topside and his assistant, an elderly man of indeterminate age who speaks only Setswana, crouch near an open fire. The truck is piled high with double mattresses, each neatly wrapped in heavy plastic, and beneath them is a stack of coir mats, fibrous coconut floor rugs, hairy and rough. The evening midges are starting to swarm and the Bell Frogs are in chorus: we're not going to get back to camp tonight. I call Sue on the hand-held radio.

"Suze, we're at the truck. *Ja*, it took forever. Listen, it's getting dark, we'll have to stay here. Yes, we're fine. I'll give you an update in the morning."

Water, of course, is abundant, but Craig and I have no food. Topside has a pocket of oranges, however. Good enough. May in the Okavango brings chilly nights, so we build up the fire. The old man is busying himself among the mattresses up on the bed of the truck.

"What's he doing, Topside?" I ask.

He flicks his head toward the darkness contemptuously, emphasising my ignorance.

"He is afraid of lions. He is making his bed up there before it becomes too dark."

"The lions won't bother us here," I say. "There are four of us, we have a fire, we're making a lot of noise, and they won't like the truck."

"They can come when we sleep. They will come!" he replies emphatically.

Superstitious fellows, I muse to myself. Why are so many Africans so afraid of African animals? You'd think they'd have got used to them by now: after all, the animals have been here since the dawn of man. I'm happy to depend on experience and a bit of luck: it's worked for me before. We settle down to our simple supper. Oranges.

The white-beard continues to fuss about up there on the truck-bed, arranging his grimy blankets, stacking mats around the edge of the load. He measures the distance from his sleeping place to the ground and, apparently satisfied, dusts off his hands, descends and joins us at the fire. I peel an orange, and casually toss the peels into the fire.

Immediately, old White-beard and Topside go ballistic! They're shouting, frantically scratching the peels out of the embers with a piece of firewood and glaring malevolently at me, very upset.

"No! No! Do not throw the peels into the fire!" shouts Topside at me.

"What?" I say, confused.

"No peels! No peels! Ai, ai, ai, ai ... " he carries on.

"What? Why not? What the hell?" I persist.

"It brings the lions! The lions will come! You are bringing the lions!"

"Rubbish, man! Topside, that's nonsense. What are you talking about?"

"It's true! Now they will come. You will see. It is known. Orange peels, when they burn, they bring the lions! And don't call me rubbish! It is not good to my culture."

He's absolutely furious with me, and now seemingly insulted too.

"I didn't say *you* are rubbish, I said you are *speaking* rubbish," I try to explain.

But semantics have no place in this argument. I have committed a grave offence. In Motswana culture, for some unknown reason, the innocuous English words "nonsense" and "rubbish" have acquired a deeply disrespectful meaning, and many is the naive *lekgoa* who has fallen unwittingly into this trap. It is pointless to argue about the true meanings of the words, and the Batswana are slow to forgive you for the blunder. My relationship with Topside has deteriorated even further now with this gaffe.

The white-beard's eyes are blazing, too, with undisguised

malevolence and no small measure of contempt. He's leaning forward, brandishing his piece of wood, the charred end smoking and spitting small sparks in all directions, clucking at me, babbling in Setswana. Craig is surreptitiously piling his orange peels to one side in the darkness, fearful of being rounded upon. I make the mistake of trying to apply some logic to the situation.

"Topside, lions have been here forever. Oranges are imported. They only arrived in this country a few decades ago, at most. They don't even grow in Botswana. Definitely not in the Okavango! How could lions associate oranges with fires?"

"It is known, this thing. We know. You have done a bad thing now. They will come," he replies with no attempt to engage me in rationale.

Fear is real, whether there is a logical foundation for it or not. Fear comes from belief. But from whence does belief stem? Tradition, for starters. It's a convoluted debate and there will be no calm reasoning around this fire tonight. Chastened, frustrated, and a bit cross, I give up. The four of us sit in uneasy silence a while longer, eating our oranges methodically, segment by segment, and carefully collecting the peels in a plastic bag so that they can later be locked away in the cab of the truck. Any marauding lions, intent on forsaking all of their evolutionary history as carnivores and swapping tonight to a fruit diet, will not detect them there, apparently. But our Motswana colleagues are in no doubt that I have now placed everyone in mortal danger. Soon, Topside and the old fellow retire to the safety of the truck, muttering to each other with much theatrical shaking of their heads. Although there is ample room atop the Henschel, Craig and I, in a perfectly deliberate show of defiance, unload a pile of the mattresses and some coir mats, and build ourselves a castle on the ground, right there on the road. One mattress flat, with four propped up around us, and another balanced on top to form a roof, all held together by thin sisal rope tied from within.

We pass a long and chilly night in our rudimentary shelter, swatting at mosquitoes and shifting uncomfortably under the scratchy mats. At length, the relief of dawn arrives, and as the redness brightens the still water and the light comes flooding across the land, a hubbub arises from the truck.

"Ai ai ai! Look, Lloyd. Look!"

"What now, Topside? God!" I exclaim sleepily.

Craig and I cut the string holding our flimsy shelter together, and the castle walls crash down with a 'whump" on to the damp *kweek* grass. Topside and the old man are staring down onto the road, blankets still wrapped about them, their eyes large in the growing light. Everywhere, everywhere about us are the fresh tracks of lions. Lions, big and small, old and young. An entire pride has walked down the road, stopped to investigate, milled about, sniffed around, rolled and lolled and then moved on.

"Jesus!" says Craig vehemently.

"They were here! You see! They were here, the lions!" shouts Topside from the safety of the truck.

Old Methuselah, the white-beard, is babbling again, alternately pointing a gnarled finger at me, remonstrating, then gesturing at the lion tracks. I sigh loudly in exasperation and some amazement.

"They weren't trying to *kill* us, Topside. They were just inquisitive. It's nothing. We were in no danger. Tell the old man not to worry. We're fine, man!"

Topside relays the message and then translates the withering response in a rancorous voice.

"He says he doesn't care about *you!* You are a young man with no children, and you know nothing. But he is a grandfather. He has five grandchildren. He wants to see them grow older. It is not you he is worried about. It is *himself!*"

9

ISAAC HAS A NARROW ESCAPE

Isaac is telling one of his stories.

"Mister Lloyd, a hippo made us fright one day. Patrick the River Bushman said, 'That hippo is totally dead. Let's sit on it. And smoke a cigarette.' Yo, yo, yo ... "

Isaac laughs a lot. He's laughing now. He's one of those congenial, good-natured men that unconsciously lifts everyone's spirits. He's poling Charlie, Lili and me in an Okavango *mekoro* across the duck-scattered floodplains of Jao towards the Baobab Island. We're in search of an elusive and rare Fishing Owl, and Isaac reckons he knows in which African Mangosteen tree one is likely to be perched.

Isaac tells a very funny story. You laugh at the *way* he tells it too, full of antic gestures and comic noises and employing his own brand of English, and I chuckle in anticipation: we're in for a treat. He misinterprets my laugh, though, because he stops the boat, leans on his *ngashi* and says:

"But Mister Lloyd, it is true. This story, it is true! It was me, Isaac, who was there that day."

"Tell us the whole story, Isaac. Everything that happened," I invite him.

"I will tell you when we reach," he says, pointing at the baobab. "First we must drink coffee."

It's a perfect May morning in the Okavango Delta. Shafts of bright sunlight thrust so deep into the clear water that you can pick out the bream as they lazily fin across the golden sand-beds. Isaac hands Charlie and Lili some coffee, the steam curling lazily from the enamel mugs, then settles on the prow of the dugout. His dazzling smile brightens the morning further. You can see he relishes telling this story.

"That morning it was me, Isaac, and Patrick the River Bushman, and my cousin. We were three. We were going to Jacana Camp. But not in the shallow water, like this. We were going there in the deeper water. The water was deeper. So we were two of us poling and one sitting. It was in the evening and the sun was only a little bit of light left."

He smiles at us, seeking our understanding, and we all nod and smile back. He goes on.

"Then we came to a place in the channel. It was a place of high reeds, this place, on both sides. The water was fast there, and the river it was small. Too small. You cannot turn the *mekoro* around there, in this place. And there was a hippo. A big hippo."

A flight of Squacco Herons flies by on curiously silent wings, and the *mekoro* rocks gently. Isaac spreads his arms, to indicate something massive. Charlie and Lili have settled on a fallen Fan palm trunk, sipping their drinks. They are safari veterans and love a well-told tale. This is one they've never heard and they're enjoying it.

"The hippo was too big," Isaac continues. "Big, like this, like the *mekoro*. It was lying across the channel. But it didn't see us because we held the reeds in our hands and we stopped and we were very quiet. But we were fearing."

He runs a hand across the front of his face, and shakes his head slowly at the memory of it.

"Big! Then Patrick the River Bushman said, '*Ai* man, this hippo is dead. See, it is just floating there. It is totally dead! Come, let us go closer: we must pass.' But my cousin and me, we said to Patrick,

'No, no, we must be careful! Perhaps it is only sleeping.' We held the reeds very tight with our hands. But Patrick the River Bushman said, '*Ai* man, let's go *munna*.' "

A sneaky wind riffles the water's surface. The hot coffee is delicious in this morning chill. Isaac gathers breath. He seems to be waiting for me to ask the obvious question. I happily oblige.

"So did you go to the hippo, Isaac?"

Isaac slowly shakes his head once more and affects a sheepish look.

"We went there to that hippo. Patrick is a River Bushman. He knows these animals. But we were very afraid. I myself, Isaac, I was not sure this hippo was totally dead. And even my cousin he was also not sure. But we went there to that big hippo, and we put the *mekoro* right next to it, there in the deeper water. And that hippo, he did not move at all, Mister Lloyd, just lying there, floating, you can't believe. And Patrick said '*Munna*, this hippo it is totally dead.' And he got on the hippo. And me and my cousin, we got on the hippo also. And we started to smoke cigarettes."

A splash punctuates Isaac's story and I glance around. It's only a Pied Kingfisher, diving for fingerlings. Lili leans forward.

"Smoke?" she gasps. "Oh, okay, so the hippo had been dead a long time, then?"

Isaac chortles, enjoying our attention and revelling in our astonishment. I laugh at his laugh, at his telling of the story.

"Missis Lili, that hippo was not there in the morning when I came. Uh uh! But now, he was there. And we were sitting on him, smoking. And we looked at his back while we were smoking and we saw there were many broken places from fighting, and blood, and some deep wounds, and we said, 'aah, this one, he has died from fighting with another male hippo, and he has died here today.' And Patrick the River Bushman took his *ngashi*, you know, this long stick for poling the *mekoro*, and we said, 'Wait Patrick, what are you going to do, don't do that!' Because he was poking the end of the stick in one of the wounds, and he said, 'I just want to make sure the hippo is totally dead.' And we were afraid again, and I said, 'Hey *munna*, don't do that! You must stop!' But then Patrick raised the *ngashi* and he hit that hippo deep into a cut on its back, he hit it too hard, but we were sitting on the hippo's back, smoking cigarettes."

Isaac's eyes are narrowed in mirth to small slits and he guffaws loudly, slapping his bare thighs. The noise scales out over the water and through the papyrus islands. A pair of Pygmy Geese, hitherto undetected among the water lilies, bursts into startled flight.

"Mister Lloyd, that hippo was only sleeping. Ai ai ai! It was not at all totally dead! And it became awake very fast. Hey, it was very angry, that one. Because we were three and we were on its back, and it did not like that. And it rose up and it roared like a lion at night, and me and Patrick and my cousin, we were thrown into the water, which was deeper there, and you know we Batswana, we cannot swim."

He draws breath.

"We cannot swim but that day we were like fishes, Mister Lloyd! And I was under the water, and all around me the water was white with the swimming also of the hippo, and there were pieces of *mekoro* everywhere because the hippo had bitten the boat into too many pieces. And I was very afraid. But I swam into the reeds and I don't know where Patrick the River Bushman and my cousin went to. And when I came up inside the reeds, I was trying to be very quiet, but my breathing it was too loud, and the hippo was gone. Totally gone. And the *mekoro* was floating in many pieces. And Patrick and my cousin, they were totally gone also."

Again, the dramatic pause and the expectant look.

"Did you find them, Isaac?" asks Charlie, his coffee cooling rapidly and long forgotten.

"Then I was very quiet there. Hippos are too clever. But then I was starting to think about crocodiles. A crocodile ate a man in our village when he went fishing and I was thinking, uh uh. So I started to go slowly by slowly towards the island, making no noises. And then I heard something, a very quiet noise from the island and it was Patrick and my cousin and they were saying – 'Isaac, Isaac, Isaac' – quietly like that. And when I reached, they said 'Oh Isaac, we thought you were dead!' "

Coppery-tailed Coucals bubble from their perches in the long grass, and catfish rise: listening to Isaac, we are worlds away from the chaos that Isaac is describing. But in Africa, you never know when it is going to break out.

"And I said to Patrick the River Bushman, 'Why did you hit the hippo with the *ngashi*, now look what has happened, and it is getting dark, and the *mekoro* is there in the channel but it is broken.' And my cousin was angry also and he said, 'Yes Patrick, now look what you have done.' But Patrick said nothing, he looked away, and then he said, 'Now we must walk, it is getting dark.' But you know, the water between the islands was deeper, and we had to walk in water to here – he indicates his waist – from island to island. Hey, we were fearing that night."

"Why didn't you just sleep there on the island and wait to be rescued the next day, Isaac?" asks Charlie.

An incredulous look passes across Isaac's face.

"No, it is dangerous! There are many lions here, too many. Uh uh. It is better to walk to the camp in the darkness, even in the water. A lion, *ai munna*, that one, no, it is better to walk, you can't wait."

I see. Lions, bad. Sitting on a not-totally-dead hippo while having a smoke, not so bad.

"But then we reached. We were too happy to get to the camp, and the people were wondering where we were, and we said, 'We are here, but there was a big *matata* (problem) with a hippo, but now we are here.' And in the morning the camp manager said, 'Isaac, you must show me this place where the hippo was, perhaps it is dying there, we must move it out of the channel with the big boat.'"

Isaac smiles another broad smile and spreads his hands, palms open.

"And I said, 'No, no, that is not a good place, it is too dangerous. I am not going back there. Because that hippo, it is not totally dead.'"

10

THE BUFFALO EVENING

Lonesome Dove is a true story about a teenager who sails single-handed around the globe in a small dinghy. Or so I had thought until the evening of the buffalos.

I love guiding at Mombo, a safari camp in the Okavango Delta. I love *living* at Mombo; a dramatic wildlife encounter seems to occur every single day. I have a sense that this may just be the best time of my life. Mombo is so game-rich, so ecologically varied, so vast. Wildlife guides are in the business of dream fulfilment and if the guests are willing I can go exploring all day, discovering new routes and secret places, observing animals as they live their natural lives, and ignoring the intrusive radio chatter from the other guides. The guests love it: they feel special, like old-time explorers, and we return exhilarated to camp at the end of the day. I search far and wide across the floodplains, investigating Jackalberry forests and palm-encircled salt islands, deliberately ranging too far for any other vehicles to reach the sightings I find, eschewing the manifold comforts of the camp, swapping the spa and the bar for the game-drive car, delighting in picnic lunches at the old Boat Station and evening gin and tonic at the Simbira Baobab. Even better, discovering places that have no name at all.

I strategise by using the guest booking schedule, scrutinizing the printed sheets eagerly when they arrive in the mailbag from the Wilderness Safaris headquarters in Maun, looking for clues. Some of the guides at Mombo prefer to drive two-nighters, folk who are there for a quick predator fix: the guiding is easy and guests are joining and leaving their Land Rovers almost every day, so the tips are frequent. But I prefer to check if there is someone, or a couple, that has booked a private safari vehicle, especially if it is for three days or more. This means that they are probably keener than most on wildlife, possibly even returning guests, and they're not at Mombo just to see its legendary predators: they will want to absorb the experience, and take their time about it. And Africa is not a place that suffers those who like to rush. These are usually great people to guide. To me, they're here for the right reasons. They are my reasons, too.

My research completed, I bag a booking – a three nighter, private car – and in the late afternoon I pick them up at the Mombo airstrip, a few kilometres from camp. My companions turn out to be Americans, Southerners, quiet people, sufficient unto themselves. I have a good feeling about them immediately.

The drone of the departing Cessna 210 fades as the pilot tips his right wing, destined for Maun.

"Folks, I've packed a box with drinks and snacks. How are you feeling? If you'd like to ... " I begin.

"We're here for the bush," the woman says firmly and pleasantly, and her husband nods as he prepares his camera and lenses.

Bingo! I've picked well. I steer the Land Rover west through the tree-line flanking the floodplains where a large herd of buffalos has been seen this morning. There's nothing like sheer numbers of animals to impress from the outset. I drive without speaking much: my guests look quietly content, reveling in being in Africa. The land needs no assistance in telling its tale tonight.

The sinking sun has glory in it yet, fading with growing rapidity, splintered into broken pink shards that land on the streams and pools of the Okavango flood. I park on a slight rise overlooking a shallow pan, and decant two glasses of very cold South African Chardonnay. Africa is a place of pure theatre, and the show begins. In a few minutes the buffalo herd appears, grazing steadily towards us. Cattle Egrets dart among their feet, snatching at grasshoppers disturbed into flight by the passing hooves. Smoky clouds of midges swarm above each animal in fantastic mini-tornados. There is a constant lowing as the calves make contact calls with their mothers. Black bulls mill around us, massive, with heavy horns and malevolent stares, their eyes red and rheumy. The buffalos, a herd at least 500-strong, splash past us through the shallow water for fully half an hour. Somewhere, a hippo grunts. We barely speak. Then as the act finishes and the buffalos exit the stage, the man says:

"Well, this puts *Lonesome Dove* in the shade."

A reader! Brilliant. I love reading, and I love talking about books with guests, in camp and on game drives. At sightings where the animal is relaxed, even asleep sometimes, book talk entertains and enlightens and rounds up the experience. If a guest finishes the book they are reading while in camp, and leaves it with me, even better. A new book in camp is a rare and treasured thing: a good book – actually, even a bad book – quickly does the rounds among the managers and guides, rapidly becoming battered and dog-eared and a topic of conversation.

"Oh, that's that book about the sailor," I say.

He exchanges an amused look with his wife.

"No son, it's about a cattle drive from Texas to Montana. Larry McMurtry. You should read it," he chuckles.

I'm a bit embarrassed. We keep watching the buffalos as they drift north along the tree line, and with the final dying of the light, I head for camp. It's been a poetic start to the safari. The tone has been set.

At dinner, the campfire is throwing crazy, leaping shadows back at the night, and we speak of books. It turns out that these folk are lawyers from Houston who spend their spare cash and time doing two things: going on safari, and collecting and reading books, including first editions. Usually, they each read their own copy of the same book at the same time so that they can discuss it as they go. I like that idea. It's unusual.

My instincts prove correct. They turn out to be wonderful people to guide, the type that take in the nuances of the wilderness and appreciate nature in its finer details. Our days together are long and slow, filled with quiet conversations about authors shared and authors unknown, leisurely picnics under spreading Sausage trees down at the river, walks among the inquisitive Lechwe antelope that dash into the safety of deeper water as we approach, while the air is alive with birdcall. It is idyllic.

After four days the little Cessna returns for them and I'm very sad to see them go. I return to the more usual routine of guiding groups of guests to lions on the kill, leopards lazing in trees and great horned Kudus, large stately antelopes, that walk quietly among the ash-grey Leadwood trees.

A month later, the mailbag produces a package for me, post-marked 'Houston, USA.' Intrigued, I tear it open. It's a fat paperback – *Lonesome Dove*!

On the inside cover of the book there is an inscription:

"The buffalo evening. From two fellow readers."

11

UNICORN OF THE MIND

I've gone and got myself *bajewed*. Badly stuck. But not in a Land Rover this time. There's no high-lift jack that will get me out of this mess. And it's all because of a stupid unicorn.

Bajewed is Shanglish, pidgin Shangaan. Guide-speak at Mala Mala Game Reserve to describe just how irrevocably stuck our Land Rover was in mud or sand. We former *lowveld* guides have brought these expressions with us to Botswana. To Mombo. As in: "*Jus, china, I was bajewed to the diff, man.*" (Jeez, my friend, I was stuck as deep as the differential, man.)

Today, I'm up to the diff again. It's an accident of my own making. Getting stuck always is. I'd rather be jammed tight in the mud in a Land Rover because this is worse than that. I am struggling in a self-spun web and I'm battling to disengage with dignity. It was just a silly little joke, a throw-away line, that's all. You smile, you give a little laugh, you move on. You'd think.

But Janice is writing down just about everything I say. Even while I'm driving, she's scratching away in her travel journal. My Land

Rover has pretty good suspension, but seriously? She's sitting directly behind me on every game drive, scribbling, her husband mute and stony-faced next to her. It pains me that he's not having a good time. Who knows why he's on safari? Her idea, I guess. Janice's dream, not his. He's probably missing some baseball series at home, or would rather be on the golf course with his friends. I think he prefers his animals on a plate with fries. Talk about stuck: poor old Bob is stuck on safari, with his wife.

Today I also have two other guests on board the game drive vehicle: Julian, a British travel writer, and his Australian fiancee, Anna. They're razor-sharp, witty, understated, well-travelled and interested. The pair of them are perched high up in the back row, a vacant row of seats between them and the Americans, and more than just the Atlantic Ocean apart in every respect. They couldn't be *more* different.

The morning is bright and very crisp and we've had an entertaining drive watching "The Steroid Boys", two big cheetahs, trying to catch some Impalas, which are common antelopes in these parts. I stop so that we can thrust aside the winter chill with a mug of coffee. I face the car towards the uniquely magical scene that the Okavango Delta provides; sparkling blue water dotted with lilies, a massive Sausage tree growing along the pool's edge, pairs of Egyptian Geese passing by, calling hoarsely, and the sound of Fish Eagles as they wheel overhead. A bachelor herd of male Red Lechwes are grazing close by, nonchalant and relaxed. We disembark. It's one of those gentle mornings on which the sun warms you subtly, and there is a calm serenity that passes understanding. You just can't get enough of it: it's like a hot shower that you cannot bring yourself to get out of.

Bob remains resolutely in the Land Rover, apparently determined not to enjoy any part of this occasion. I pass the chipped green enamel mugs around. We lean against the Land Rover fender, dipping hard, dry rusks into our coffee, quietly appreciating this moment. Janice breaks the silence.

"What are those deer, Leon?" she asks, pointing.

I sigh inwardly. It's Lloyd, but never mind. And these are by no means the first Lechwes we have seen. In fact, we stopped at a different herd only twenty minutes ago, and we discussed them at length: how their hooves are elongated to cope with soggy conditions underfoot, why there are no females with them at this time of the season, various ways of avoiding being eaten by hungry predators, even, in some detail, the fact that they are not deer at all, but antelopes. Those are horns, not antlers. And no, these are not Impalas: those were the ones that the cheetahs were hunting this morning, remember? All this has already been faithfully transcribed, of course, the sound of the short pencil squeaking as my words are recorded in The Little Black Safari Book. I'm a bit frustrated and I momentarily let my guard down.

"Those are Red Lechwes. Except for that one, you see that one there with the single horn, Janice? That one is a unicorn!"

My reply is deliberately flippant, my tone light: it's just banter. Many antelopes break off one of their horns while fighting with other males during the rut, which leaves them with only half their weaponry and a lop-sided look. To be fair, we have passed a few Impalas this morning with a single horn, too. Julian and Anna smile a little and Bob ignores me. But my attempt at humour misses the mark with Janice.

"Unicorn? Gosh!" she exclaims.

I make the mistake of thinking that she is playing along.

"Oh, yes," I say gaily. "But *this* one is a Swamp Unicorn. Endemic to the Okavango, of course. Brilliant sighting this, really special."

"So what other kinds of unicorns do you get?" she asks.

The pencil is squeaking again. Okay, cool, she gets it, I think. Good. Enthusiastically, I continue to dig myself in.

"Well, there's the Desert Unicorn of Namibia, never seen one of those unfortunately – very rare. And then you get the South African Mountain Unicorn, quite common if you know where to look, those are the first ones I ever saw. I must have been only five or six, but I'll never forget it."

I grin at my own joke, but then I look at Bob. He is as still and silent as granite, and obviously angry with me for apparently making fun of his wife. This little prank is no laughing matter to him.

Where many partners might step in to rescue the situation with an, "Oh, my dear, he's just teasing you, it's a little joke", Bob does not. Now that I'm up to the proverbial differentials, he's glowering at me in censure. He has no word of comfort for Janice, though. I'm embarrassed, and quite surprised at him, actually. Janice is still writing. I try to rescue the situation.

"Um, Janice, sorry, I'm just kidding, it's not a unicorn, you know, it's only a Lechwe with a single horn. You remember we spoke about that?" I explain weakly.

Just twenty short minutes ago, I think to myself. You wrote it down for goodness sake. She stops writing, and looks up at me. A look of childlike confusion crosses her face.

"But what about the other ones, the Desert Unicorns and the Mountain Unicorns, then?" she asks.

Surely … no, I must put a stop to this. Now.

"No, no, no," I start to explain.

This comes out a little too loudly. Steady on, Campo, I tell myself. Be gentle. Contritely, I say:

"No. Sorry Janice, I was only teasing you. There's no such thing as a unicorn at all. It's a fable."

With a look of hurt reproach, Janice bends back to her book and with careful deliberation draws a line through the notes she has just written. I see with a huge pang of remorse that she had even started to sketch her "unicorn", and this drawing too now begins to disappear under the cruel diagonal lines of the pencil. It breaks my heart. Bob sits immutable in his strange triumph, apparently happy to let me squirm. I walk around the vehicle to Janice and put a hand on her shoulder. She's gazing at the Lechwes now, disillusioned.

"So, Leon, are you saying that all unicorns are just made-up animals?" she asks.

"Made-up animals." That's how she phrases it. Suddenly this situation is more than embarrassing: it's sad. Janice is sixty-six, going on ten. The enormity of her child-like naïveté and disappointment engulfs me in a wave of guilt. I resolve instantly that for the rest of the safari she (and for her sake, her husband too) is going to get very special, exceedingly patient attention from me and that every single thing she sees from this point on will have a special glow of magic about it.

Because after all, why *can't* this be a unicorn? *Her* unicorn. All of us treasure a unicorn of the mind, and have one tucked away somewhere.

12

DOWN AT THE
BOAT STATION

"There they are! There they are! Lloyd! Lloyd!"

I know. I can't miss them. I hadn't envisaged the search culminating in quite this way, but still. My khaki trousers are around my ankles, which is awkward.

This is my favourite area of Mombo: the Red Lechwe-littered expanses of short open grassland down at the Boat Station. Looking out towards Xigera across the white and silver water, you can see for miles. The game viewing right across the Mombo concession is legendary, the sought-after predators usually so close to camp, even occasionally *in* camp, that hardly any of the guides bother to come down here. They don't need to. So if you fancy an adventure and want to go exploring, you will usually have this neck of the woods all to yourself. It requires some nerve to venture this far from camp with new guests on board, though: most guides are too nervous to be out of radio range of the other vehicles in case something exciting is discovered. It makes afternoon tea complicated when the morning drive's sightings are compared and your guests find that they missed seeing the wild dogs that were resting, fat and full, under the ebony tree up at Paradise Plains because on a whim you chose to check out the opposite end of the concession area.

These days the annual winter flood is quite moderate compared to times past, which allows us to plunge the game-drive vehicle through shallow water crossings and access the far-flung reaches of the area, driving south-west across the hippo-grazed plains, winding around the numerous palm-fringed islands that harbour shy Bushbuck, and stretch out finally to the sandy expanses along the creeping fingers of the Boro river. Here, herds of zebras ceaselessly whisk their tails as they feed in company with graceful Impalas and Blue Wildebeest upon the coarse, salty grass. For all of us guides, it is a place akin to heaven: along the watery edges are gathered small flocks of placid Knob-billed Ducks, Black Egrets with unlikely yellow feet and lapwings of several varieties. It is not uncommon to discern even at a distance the form of a leopard at ease on one of the great horizontal branches of a free-standing Sycamore Fig.

Kathy and Frank have brought their grandchildren to Africa, just as long ago they promised me they would, and they are the right people for an adventurous outing: willing to take a risk, not much concerned about seeing what everyone else has seen. They understand that the payoff can be huge. Because if we do find something amazing this morning, we will be alone down here at the Boat Station. It will be a private sighting, just us and the brisk, wild wind. All the other guides seem to have gone north this morning, and I have switched my game-drive radio off. Freedom! Freedom from the hiss and click of the radio, the incessant broken chatter; freedom from the requirement to tick off every sighting and to call in other guides to the wonderful things that I hope to find. The kitchen staff is going to hate me, of course. We're going to be late for brunch again, but my view is that these guests can eat glorious food at any hotel or restaurant in the world. Food is not what they came here for. It's this. This!

"They can be fabulous, the lion sightings down at the Boat Station, if you can find them," I told the family earlier. "There are some big boys down there. Let's give it a go!"

I had guided Kathy and Frank years ago at Mala Mala in South Africa and we had stayed in touch, writing Christmas cards to each other for years. Now they're back with me in a game-drive vehicle, but this time in Botswana, and with Barney and Jackie. It has already been an excellent few days with plenty of joking and banter; they're good people. It can be difficult to hold a teenager's attention on safari: sometimes they don't yet have the maturity to appreciate what an opportunity they have been given, and would really rather be hanging out with their friends at the beach. Not Barney and Jackie, though: they're loving it. And we've seen great stuff: "The Steroid Boys", legendary Mombo cheetahs on the hunt; a den of tiny jackal pups; twenty-six male giraffes gathered unusually together on Goss' Plains; an African Fish Eagle snatching a gasping catfish from the water's surface. Strangely, though, very few lions.

Which is why we are here this morning. To locate the two big fellows that dominate this area; they're magnificent: mature dark-maned males, in their prime but frustratingly reclusive. I really want to find them for these kids. They're so keen and interested. They deserve them. Though it's not going to be easy down at the Boat Station, it's worth a shot: it's quite hard to track animals in these sands where the integrity of the *spoor* is soon lost and the wiry *kweek* grass doesn't hold the sign. No-one has seen these two lions for ages. Are they even still in the concession or have other lions perhaps driven them out? Even if we don't find them, it's a scenic, leisurely drive, glorying in the majesty of the Okavango wilderness.

"Folks, there's absolutely no sign of these guys," I'm forced to admit eventually when we reach our destination. "No early morning roaring, no tracks, no dung, no vultures gathered on trees indicating a kill. They're like ghost lions. But it's beautiful down here, isn't it?"

It truly is, but is that really enough, I wonder? I watch the sandy road ahead of me as I drive, but I see only the tracks of hippos, antelopes, Spotted Hyenas, the occasional elephant. Even the Kudus, slow-running antelope whose best defence is to hide in thick bush, are walking without concern across the sweeping grassland. Every creature is at peace. The sun is gentle and soothing, slowly nudging the June chill aside, casting soporific warmth on our cheeks, and I'm feeling comfortably drowsy.

I also need to go to the toilet quite urgently. I've been putting it off for an hour, not wanting to lose any good early-morning tracking time, and now it has become a pressing need. I stop the Land Rover on the edge of a spreading shallow lagoon where African Jacanas skitter across the water's surface and poke about on the floating water-lily leaves. A small herd of Impalas looks up at us without much interest, then continues grazing.

"Right, everyone out. We've earned a coffee and a muffin. Give me a few minutes; I'll be just behind that clump of Date palms," I announce.

They chuckle a little, and Frank extracts a new toilet roll and a brown paper bag from the seat pocket and tosses them playfully at me.

"Rather you than me, pal," he laughs. "I'll wait till we're back at camp."

This is an old joke. They all find it rather embarrassing and unusual to go to the toilet in the bush, and try to avoid doing so. Jackie is a little bit precious about it, feigning shock: she doesn't want to deal with putting the used paper into the brown bag and carrying it back to camp with us. But toilet paper takes ages to break down and looks unsightly and unnatural out here; it's bad practice and poor ethics to leave it out in the bush. Some guests prefer to hang on grimly until they get back to the lodge, but not me. I prefer the "loo with a view."

The family disembarks, all wrapped in their game-drive blankets to ward off the cold. I set up the little refreshment table, pour coffee and dispense oat crunchie cookies and while their mugs warm their hands, I walk hurriedly over to the dense palm thicket, the roll of "White Gold" clasped in my hand. I'll feel less distracted after this. I want my focus to be on the lions: I know they're here somewhere. Maybe after coffee I'll drive over to the Simbira Baobab, following the channel edge. Surely they haven't crossed over towards Xigera: Okavango lions can and do swim, but isn't the water way too deep out in that direction? That's why there used to be a boat stationed here after all. No.

They're here, these lions. Somewhere close.

Hidden behind the palm coppice, I toss my fleece jacket across a convenient tree trunk. It flaps there emptily, vacant and strange. There are numerous low entrance tunnels beneath the palms, created by the passage of animals. I choose an opening and settle down, facing the lagoon, the paper bag and the toilet roll beside me. Barney's laugh reaches me, the result of some small joke that Jackie has just told – they're still amused at the thought of me squatting here, probably. Blacksmith Lapwings are wheeling by in a tizzy, scolding us for disturbing them. It's a beautiful morning.

Crouching there, a different noise gains my attention, something low and out of place and unexpected, cutting though the shrill whistling of the lapwings and the dry rattling of the palm fronds. That's funny. What was that? Some-one stirs more sugar into their coffee and I hear the sound of the spoon tinkling against the mug. Then there it is again: a sustained grumble, but growing louder. It's hard to ascertain where it is coming from. Surely not behind me?

A slow realisation blossoms, swiftly replaced by a feeling of awful dread. Helpless and immobile, with my trousers around my ankles, armed only with a roll of recycled, environmentally friendly, two-ply toilet paper, I slowly twist around. The tunnel penetrates deep into a gloomy central grotto. There is nothing to be seen. But the sound comes again, a low and menacing growl. And with immediate and blinding certainty I know what I'm hearing: lions.

This is very awkward indeed. I cannot run even if I want to. At best I could manage a frantic hop. No, I need to stay very still and brazen this out. I still can't see the lions but the growling is becoming fiercer. Especially at point-blank range, it is a low and perilous sound and I feel utterly exposed. I realise that I have entirely lost the urge to go to the toilet. You're going to have to roll the dice, fellas, I think. Please be nice.

And so I squat there, presenting these apex predators with my naked backside. This is behaviour they have never encountered before. Most potential prey would at least attempt to run away, but I have remained there, apparently unafraid. For several long seconds a stalemate prevails. Then their nerve cracks.

With an almighty explosive "woof" the two lions come bounding out of the palm grove, streaking in full horrified flight down a parallel passageway, thundering their discontent, sprinting out onto the plain. They run for about a hundred metres and then wheel about, ears flattened, tails whipping behind them, staring hard at me. I am still paralyzed, still down on my haunches. In their confusion, the lions are magnificent and comical in equal measure. It is quite funny to see them off-balance like this. Despite my own shock, I can't help but laugh out loud. Never have these kings of beasts been treated with such apparent disdain, and they're rattled.

Then comes Frank's frantic shout:

"There they are! There they are! Lloyd! Lloyd!"

I know. Thanks! I'm giggling crazily with a mixture of fear and relief. Dragging my pants up, I re-emerge from behind the palms. Kathy and Frank are up in the Land Rover now, pointing at the lions, looking out for me and yelling my name. Coffee mugs lie strewn on the grass; the blankets lie abandoned in tangled heaps. The amazed Impalas are stamping their forelegs, ears cocked forwards, making sharp alarm snorts. Barney and Jackie are sheltering with wide eyes behind the car, Jackie still with a crunchie half way to her mouth. It is very funny.

The two lions start to recover their dignity. Casting a last lingering suspicious look at me, they begin the most decorous retreat they can muster. As do I. I calmly rescue a mug from the ground and pour myself some coffee. The four Americans are staring at me, bemused.

"Well, there you go friends, that's how we do it," I say. "It's pretty good, the lion viewing, down here at the Boat Station."

13

HAMSTRUNG

I just can't help feeling that I'm about to do some urgent running again.

There's definitely something in the air, something intangible and ominous. A distant part of my brain is sending a warning signal but the little red flashing light is dull and remote. It's making me vaguely uneasy but my wits are foggy from a combination of not enough sleep, biting cold and too much alcohol, and the brain synapses aren't quite connecting.

Then something moves in the darkness, and I think, "Oh hell, here we go again!"

It was great fun around the fire last night, laughing and swapping stories with the guests in camp, the new ones in room two. Interesting people. And they do like a whisky.

"ABF?" I kept asking. They were really into it. "Absolutely bloody final? One for the road?"

"Rude not to," they'd replied.

Now it's another bitterly cold Mombo morning, and since I was on duty last night I'm up again very early to do the wake-up calls and kick-start the camp into life; that's the system here. I'm thinking about which guests need waking, which are sleeping in, who needs an early transfer to the airstrip, which guide is picking up the freight delivery, all the usual daily logistics of running a bush camp. Funny though, I could have sworn I felt the tent shaking a little at some time in the night, the entire deck upon which it is built moving gently, rhythmically. Could that be? Just a whisky dream, I suppose.

The day is slow to arrive this morning. An unseasonal low and threatening cloud hangs over the eastern horizon, moodily holding the first rays of light at bay. In the gloom I have reluctantly rolled out of bed, dashed water across my sleep-creased face, and pulled on the rumpled khaki clothing from last night. A thick woollen beanie is dragged down well over my ears, I don gloves and a heavy coat, and I stumble onto the veranda. Duty calls, and the guests need to begin their next exciting day in the Botswana wilderness. I am longing for that first cup of java around the robust blaze of the living fire. I will stand with my back to the flames, holding the squat tin mug in both hands to warm them, and in that rare moment of peaceful solitude before the eager guests arrive, I will savour the coffee, listen to the last descending hoots of the tiny Barred Owlet and watch the first diagonal pillars of the sun begin to cast gentle peach hues onto the still waters of the creeping Okavango flood. It is always, always, worth being up for that.

But first it's a familiar morning routine. I feel quietly on the bedside table for my heavy flashlight, trying not to disturb Sue. The door makes that annoying low scraping noise that it does every winter as I push it open. I press the switch of the flashlight: it emits only a brief, dull orange glimmer, and then fades to black. Damn it! The batteries have gone flat, and the replacements are up at the office. This isn't good: it's as dark as a Welsh coal mine. My wristwatch throws an eerie green glow, reading 05h25. Five minutes to wake-up call, and I have to go. The staff tents are built on low platforms but are not connected to the camp by raised wooden walkways, so to get to the guests' rooms I have to follow a narrow dirt path, navigating between trees and clumps of low, scrubby bush. And it is *so* dark out there this morning.

I step off the veranda and start to move blindly towards the walkway, but it's okay, I know the path well. In broad daylight it's a mere two-minute walk. Sleepily, I set off, that first coffee on my mind.

I have only walked about thirty metres when I begin to feel strangely apprehensive. Something is amiss. What is that smell? It's a familiar, earthy ... oh my God! Buffalo! I freeze, all at once fully awake. The reek is so close. I stare hard into the last dregs of the night, rattled. It's likely to be a *dagga boy*, one of those massive, near-sighted, short-tempered bulls – old men that wander alone or in small groups, formidable warriors that even lions tend to steer clear of. But buffalos are black, impossible to see in this light, especially when they are lying on their bellies, chewing the cud after their night grazing, watching and waiting. He's extremely close to me but making no sound at all. All I can hear is muted chatter and the distant clink of crockery over at the kitchen where the staff are preparing the coffee and baking the croissants. It seems a long way from here this morning; this ordinary path has taken on epic proportions. Unexpectedly, I have found myself in buffalo country.

My sole consolation is that apparently the *dagga boy* is unaware of my presence. So far. I slide a boot cautiously forward, squinting hard into the shadows, willing on the early light. A working flashlight would be useful right about now. At present its only possible function is as a small club, which will be of no use against an aggrieved half-ton buffalo. Then my boot crushes a small twig. It snaps loudly.

An abrupt bovine grunt erupts next to me and an immense presence lurches to its hooves with frightening speed. That too-familiar chill engulfs me. The buffalo is terrifyingly close and the smell and sound of him is overwhelming and horrifying. In the dim illumination of the very first light, I can just make him out: mercifully, he has his back to me, the curved horns facing away, the great head swinging from side to side, looking for the source of this disturbance. A momentary relief floods through me and a plan takes shape: it's only another fifty metres to the stairs of the walkway, the buffalo is facing the other way – I'm going to have to run for it.

But then I see that it is a ... female buffalo. This is even bigger trouble. Females and their calves usually congregate in large herds, accompanied by some bulls. This accounts for the unusually strong manure smell. There must be *dozens* of them here. Very close.

In this moment the light strengthens a little, and there they are. I'm still rooted to the spot, trying to decide whether to run forwards or backwards, when all around me the herd begins to come awake, roused by the sound of the female I have stirred up. In a second, patches of shadow transform themselves into 500 kilogram buffalos, shaking themselves upright, making explosive mooing sounds as they find their legs, rising from the brown earth and shaking the dried grass from their hides, looking about them with curious eyes. They are everywhere but the steps are close. Sanctuary lies within grasp. In a split-second I make up my mind. There is no future in standing here. I run!

I sprint in the frigid air for all I am worth, without drawing breath, my boots thundering, my coat flapping, dodging around buffalos, leaping over the rump of one that lies yet on the path, side-stepping a red-brown calf that lurches from behind a shrub, willing myself on in panicked flight through the herd. I'm as fast as I have ever been, yet my passage to safety seems to take a lifetime, and as I take that final leap to the stairs, hoping that I won't miss it in the half-light, an old bull emerges from beneath the walkway to see what the fuss is about, the dawn glinting on his mighty crescent horns. He sees me and lifts his great head, staring in confusion down the length of his nose, but I am too quick for him. I lunge for the stairs, and make it.

Not a single buffalo has yet understood what is happening except this old patriarch, but he's taking no chances in the face of this bizarre behaviour. He goes bawling down the path towards the grassland in front of my tent, towards the open floodplain and safety. The entire herd follows in a massed, confused, bellowing rabble, threading through the trees and scrub, issuing on both sides of the tent towards the grassland. And now I see two or three *dagga boys* rapidly emerging from beneath my tent too. So it *was* they that set us a rockin': scratching their leathery old hides against the platform at night, divesting themselves of ticks and dried up mud, and mixing into my dreams.

Sue appears on the tent veranda, hastily wrapped in a dressing gown, her hair tousled, looking confused and wondering, her flashlight probing the remaining darkness. Dust from the charging herd hangs in a low curtain, slow to settle in the chilly air. Her beam finds me on the steps and I wave with false nonchalance: I'll tell her later. She shrugs and goes back to bed. For her, it's just the start of another day in Africa.

But I am on the top stair, triumphant and, I think, unscathed. Adventure has come unusually early today. I take my first step towards the rooms to start the wake-up calls – and drop like a man shot. Searing, white-hot pain screams up the back of both my upper legs and I grasp at the railings as I fall, but miss, and tumble in a clatter upon the planking, groaning in pain. For an instant I can't understand what has happened. There is a lot to deal with before the rising of the sun today.

But then I remember: I have once before experienced this, on a wet Saturday afternoon at a school rugby game when I came onto the field as a replacement without warming up. I was passed the ball as I took the field, and set off at best speed for the try-line. Bam! Down! My moment of glory was brutally cut short by an immediate and crippling injury; both hamstrings were pulled simultaneously. My teammates gave me a slow, sarcastic handclap as I was helped from the field. The embarrassment (and pain) was acute.

And here I am again, prone, gasping, useless, clutching at my thighs, eyes squeezed closed, feeling at once relieved and foolish. Footsteps approach down the walkway and I look up. It's the new folk from room two, awakened by the stampeding buffalo, dressed and ready for the day, only to find their indomitable guide lying before them, moaning, stricken. They peer down at me.

"*Ko ko*. Wake up call," I gasp.

14

TOUCHED

Courage. We wonder if we'll find it in ourselves when the time comes. We think we probably will, but it's impossible to know. And dreams. We wonder whether we will ever fulfil them, whether we have the courage to. Or empathy. Have we space enough in our hearts for others?

For each of us, the day of reckoning eventually arrives. For Jake Jerome, it came in a small forest glade on an early afternoon in Central Africa. Because of a Mountain Gorilla.

Uganda. I'm in the wonderfully named Bwindi Impenetrable National Park and Jake Jerome is on safari with me. He's seventy-nine years old but has more vim and brio than almost any client I have guided. A vibrant and questioning mind, and an easy sense of humour that makes him one of those gems in a group, he's the kind of traveller that everyone loves to be with. He's been in the corporate world, he's started his own business, he loves to cook, and he's read everything you've heard of. Jake's the dream client that makes the job easy, the client who you really look forward to sharing dinner with, the client from whom you learn things.

"I want to travel in Jake's car today," says Sarah to me.

She too is a lovely person, bubbling with enthusiasm, and she and Jake have struck a chord on this trip. We have two safari vehicles and there's always a bit of competition as to who sits where and with whom. It requires constant management.

We're off to find the Rushegura group of Mountain Gorillas in the clammy highland forests, and the park rangers down at the assembly point have told me that it will be an all-day walk. This is not good news for Jake. He's confided in me that it has been his life-long dream to see the remaining Mountain Gorillas, but that he has bad arthritis of the right hip that troubles him severely, especially on uphills. Bwindi is all about uphill slogging along liana-strewn jungle trails, fighting your way over fallen trees and through thick bush. The park rangers uses machetes to hack a way through for us when we leave the main paths. But Jake has asked me not to tell the rest of the group about his affliction, and as far as they know he is as fit as a fiddle. However, I have watched him walking on the relatively even ground of Kibale National Park when we were tracking chimpanzees this past week, and although he made it to the apes, we had to drive a vehicle along an ancient forest track to pick him up. I told everyone it was because the rain was threatening and we needed to hurry back to the lodge before the roads degenerated into a quagmire. They can't tell, but Jake has been walking in pain.

He and I had a private chat last night, and he asked that I not allow him to slow the group down. It can be a tricky business getting to the gorillas: they are highly mobile from first light, feeding through the forest, moving at pace, so the rangers try to get us to them while they are taking a digestive nap in the late morning. Timing is everything: if you find them too soon it's almost impossible to keep up with them, and if you get there too late they may have moved so far from their overnight nests that it becomes a very long and sweaty day, exhausting for most clients, who usually over-estimate their fitness.

The acid test is the eighty-odd steps from the car park at our lodge, Gorilla Forest Camp, to the reception area. I always wait at the top of the steps and observe the clients' faces and listen to their breathing so that I can judge who I will be needing to take extra care of when we trek into the forest the next day.

"Jake, listen," I had said. "I know it hurts, but you handled those steps pretty well today. You're more physically able than most people I have guided here. Do you think that if you take a few pain-killers you'll manage tomorrow?"

"Son," he'd replied. "I'm telling you, if it was just those steps, hallelujah. But how much walking is there going to be tomorrow? Plenty, right? So let's give it a go, and I'll cry off when I can't go on. Okay? I don't want to dampen the occasion for the rest of the group. I'll call it when I need to stop."

"You've travelled all the way here, Jake," I'd persisted. "You're *in* your dream. We are on the brink of seeing the gorillas, man! It's as important to me as to you that you get there. I won't fail you. In twenty-four hours you'll have your pictures, your memories, you'll be at the bar with an ice-cold Nile Special celebrating your success, celebrating the survival of a magnificent species. You'll see."

Jake had raised a sceptical eyebrow. But I already had a plan.

So this morning we make our way, a short walk, to the ranger's station to be briefed on our trek. Sarah trails along with Jake (who I have armed with two stout walking poles), chatting animatedly, and Jake is smiling, allowing her excitement to wash through him. Everyone loves Jake: he's become a legend, a talisman in our group, and they want to be in his presence.

We crowd into the safari car, a confusion of boots and sticks and day packs crammed with raingear, cameras and lunch, and set off for the forest access point. Jake is a delight – positive, joking, his usual self. He has obviously committed himself to a good effort today and is leaving the rest to the universe.

But the Rushegura gorillas are far away today, and it's a sultry day in July. We set off, Jake up front setting a comfortable pace along village paths through the banana and tea plantations that skirt the park. But as soon as we enter the forest the going becomes uneven, the footing unpredictable, and the pace slows. It's difficult for most westerners to manage the jungle: they are accustomed to flat pavement, predictable ground, moving escalators and lifts, surfaces where they don't have to pick their feet up, and plenty of head space. Uncomplicated walking. But in Bwindi it's slippery, there are countless hanging branches which continually knock their hats off, and they are constantly stumbling into logs and stones. It exhausts them, picking themselves up all day long. They each have a porter, however – a local village teenager smartly dressed in a grey uniform and rubber boots. At first the clients are too proud to accept help and they resist this luxury, but I persuade them to pay the paltry five dollar porterage fee. It's good for the local economy and – although they don't know it yet – very soon they will be utterly dependent on this agile youngster who will not only carry their daypack but, more importantly, and with infinite patience, will push, pull and support them through the thick undergrowth. The clients quickly lose their embarrassment at accepting help. Soon names are exchanged and a relationship forms.

After an hour of gallant jungle trudging, and with the prospect of many more ahead, Jake suddenly stops. Even though the other clients are also struggling, he is nevertheless slowing the group down, reducing our chances of reaching the gorillas, and he knows it.

"Come on Jake," says Sarah. "Please. Keep going. We can go as slowly as you want. Take a break whenever you need to."

But his face is drawn with pain. Jake's secret is out. The others agree that we should wait, but there is misgiving in their expressions. They are torn between loyalty to Jake and their own ambitions of seeing one of the world's iconic large mammals, and there's a bit of murmuring towards the rear of the echelon. But Jake has reached his own decision.

"Nope. You youngsters go on. I'll go slowly back with my porter. He and I have become buddies! I'll see you back at the car. Show me your pictures when you get back to the lodge. It's fine. I'm okay."

It's time to make my play. I wag a playful finger at him.

"Jake, you're part of the team and we're not leaving you behind. The apes are only a couple of hours ahead of us and you *will* see them today," I lecture him.

Jake starts to protest, and again some discontent is apparent from some in the group. They don't want to miss their chance. But they're not party to my plan.

"I beg you to improve your speed," says the head ranger, looking at his watch.

I nod, and his shrill whistle pierces the forest. Grins break out among the porters. They are in on the game, and they instinctively respect this old guy for his courage and humour. There is the sound of rubber boots running up the jungle trail, accompanied by laughter, and four extra porters emerge from the gloom, carrying long poles, a blanket and ropes. Rapidly they create a basic stretcher, gently take Jake's sweater from his astonished grasp and lay it down as a pillow. The entire process has taken no longer than a minute.

"Please sir, you are to lie down. Therefore we can extend ahead," they instruct him courteously.

I love the quaint use of English here: it's charming and strangely archaic. They extend their palms to Jake, inviting him to recline. Jake starts to protest, but I point at the stretcher.

"You know the deal Jake," I say. "We're all in this together."

Sarah is having a happy little cry, and the rest of the group are all smiles, relieved at the elegant solution and pleased for the old man. Jake puts up a token resistance but he can see that I have left him no option, and he surrenders, lying down with his hands crossed on his chest.

"How can I say no to these wonderful people?" says Jake. "I feel like I'm being put away, but at least I'll die happy."

And off they go, away up the trail at twice the speed we can manage, Jake recumbent and merrily waving his hat, until they disappear around a corner in the forest. The rest of us trudge on, but faster now, eager to catch up to the apes while they are snoozing. And after forty-five minutes, we do. Suddenly, there's Jake: he's sitting on a fallen tree, with a finger held to his lips, pointing into the bush, his face alive with anticipation. He's desperate to go into the sighting, and he is visibly excited.

"I can hear them," he says animatedly. "They're in there. You can hear them eating and farting and talking to each other!"

He laughs happily. But he has no idea yet just how much better this is about to get.

"Let us progress, please," our ranger tells us, and we move forward through the leaves.

And miraculously, there they are. At first they are indeterminate black shapes, hard to make out among the vegetation, but then a youngster bursts out, chuckling, closely followed by a second. They frolic together, rolling and tumbling, and are gone.

"Oh my God!" gasps Sarah, captivated.

The clients are in raptures, firing their cameras wildly, taking the worst but the best shots in the world; their gorilla pictures, at last. A silverback, the big man, the leader of the family, is lying on his huge tummy, watching us through amber eyes, his chin resting on his closed fist. Poignantly, he is staring at Jake, who alone of all the clients is not taking photographs. Jake is sitting quietly in the undergrowth, at peace, contentedly gazing back at the big fellow. Silverback to silverback. I watch the two of them. I recognise that this is a special moment and it pleases me immensely. Without taking his eyes off Jake, the silverback suddenly rolls to his feet, and deliberately ambles towards him, his massive head swinging.

"No look him, no look him," whispers the ranger urgently. "Come to me!"

We have been told that we may not approach closer than seven metres to the apes, and must not challenge them in any way. The ranger is very anxious and wants Jake to give way but it's all happening too fast and the 150 kilogram gorilla crosses the gap in just a few seconds. But there is no malice in his sway-backed bearing, and his leathery face is peaceful. Jake shows no fear at all. This is business between two elder statesmen, and we are not invited to the meeting.

The head ranger starts to move towards Jake, but I hold him by the arm.

"*Bwana Mkubwa,*" I say in a low voice, pointing at the two old men. "They just want to talk. No problem. Everything's okay."

The silverback stops in front of Jake and sits. We all watch, enthralled. The only noises are the calls of forest birds high in the canopy. Jake lowers his eyes at last, and now I realise for the first time that he has been touching his hip, slowly and unconsciously massaging it. The gorilla reaches out with his left hand, extends one great finger, and gently places it empathetically on the painful area.

This is Jake's reckoning. He looks up again and meets the silverback's eyes. Very quietly, but in a voice that carries across the clearing, he murmurs:

"Yes, it does hurt, my friend. But it was worth it. Thank you for allowing me to visit today. I have been waiting all my life to meet you."

15

LIGHTS OUT

The chef in his blue-checked trousers and tall white mushroom hat is lying dead still, on his back in the dirt of the car park. There is not a staff member to be seen, but their terrified shrieking still hangs in the desert air.

Paul had told me that we would need a very dramatic demonstration to underline his lessons, something memorable, otherwise the training would be a waste of time. I had agreed – but this is more than I had reckoned on.

Paul is part of the training team that I manage. As an ex-fireman, he has been seconded to run training programmes on fire prevention in the lodges, and to teach our staff how to deal with conflagrations if they occur. Safari lodges usually depend on butane gas for water heating and cooking, and often soak their wooden walkways in teak oil, which in unusual circumstances can be flammable, so this is a sensible precaution. He and I have travelled down from HQ in Windhoek, Namibia's capital city, to the lodge in a white Toyota *bakkie* loaded with shiny red fire-extinguishers. The theory part of the training is complete, and the Nama staff appear to have taken note, asking good questions and gasping in wonderment at some of Paul's stories and statistics.

"*Jis meneer, wragtig?*" (Wow, sir, really?) they exclaimed in awe as Paul regaled them with tales of just how easy it is to burn down a lodge with a carelessly discarded cigarette, an oil-soaked mop or a gas pipe gnawed through by mice. And they all know the truth of this: several lodges in Namibia have been lost to fire in this way.

But now Paul and I come to the dramatic part of the training: the practical. He explains to the gathered crowd that it is important to separate chemicals in the storerooms. The swimming pool chlorine powder should always be kept apart from the brake fluid, for example. If combined, they react by bursting into flames.

The Namas are impressed by this science until Paul pours a measure of chlorine into a plastic mineral water bottle, adds just a few drops of brake fluid, closes the lid ... and nothing happens. Paul sighs in disappointment, places the bottle on the ground behind him with a frown and switches our attention to dealing with liquid fuel fires. A forty-four gallon diesel drum, sawn in half, sits empty in the kitchen car park where the demonstration is taking place. I fill it with ten litres of diesel, the trainees crowd around and Paul lights a match and tosses it casually into the drum. Pandemonium ensues! Thirty staff members take to their heels, shouting and wailing. Paul and I remain at our posts, and when the staff find that no fire has ensued and returns, he explains that diesel cannot combust in this way. He lights the entire match box and throws it in, one foot casually up on the drum's edge. The diesel does not ignite. Paul's loving this. A few of the more courageous Namas overcome their suspicion and venture forward. I add a few litres of petrol, which floats in a green-blue sheen on the surface of the diesel. Paul invites an intrepid housekeeper closer and asks her to throw in a lit match. From a distance of several metres, she takes good aim and gingerly tosses it in.

Whoosh! The petrol lights immediately in a rush of flame, and after a few seconds it heats up the diesel, and that then also ignites in a sheet of heat and dense smoke. Startled staff members run for the cover of the kitchen once again, and when the smoke dies down, the housekeeper is still standing there, ashen and open-mouthed, wringing her hands in her apron.

"*Ai meneer, ek het gedog ek is dood!*" (Oh sir, I thought I was dead!), she says, aghast.

We invite everyone closer again, and discuss the lessons learned, and all agree in a suitably sombre tone that liquid fuels, especially petrol, are not materials to be toyed with. The lodge manager, Charles, nods in agreement: only a few weeks ago he had to transport a maintenance man suffering from severe burns to the clinic in the closest village of Maltahohe, the result of his having used siphoned petrol to light a staff fire to ward off the winter cold. Charles's face is signalling "I hope you have learned something, people" but he doesn't look all that hopeful.

It's time for the next demonstration: how to use a fire extinguisher. Everyone loves this part of the training: they're like kids with new toys. All the staff re-gather in the car park, eager to play. Paul shows them how to clear the hose nozzle of mudwasp nests, shake the powder free in the cylinder, pull the pin and hoist the extinguisher. It's a multi-stage process and hopefully in an emergency the people will remember all of them before attempting to douse a fire. I fire up the diesel/petrol mix again, and a brave young guide, Petrus, needing to re-assert some dignity after his hasty exit in the previous demonstration, moves in and extinguishes the flames with cool aplomb.

"Okay," says Paul, "well done. You're good at this. Let's see what you can do about putting out a gas fire."

Petrus grins: his reputation is restored, and he's enjoying the admiring looks of the new young waitress just in on probation from Maltahohe. But Alvis the chef steps forward, newly emboldened, shown up by the guide and no longer content to hide with the others behind the kitchen wall.

"I want to do it," he proclaims.

He is senior to Petrus, who unwillingly gives way. I roll a forty-eight kilogram gas cylinder over to Paul and he discards the cellophane dust wrapper from the brass top fitting, and turns the stopcock full open. A hush falls over the crowd as he fingers another matchbox.

This trick I have seen before and I am anticipating the fun. The gas hisses threateningly, invisibly, from the valve into the still winter morning. Suddenly Paul strikes a match, holds it in the gas stream and with a huge roar a jet of flame is instantly streaking from the nozzle, a metre long comet's tail, loud and terrifying. Paul is nonchalantly standing with his hand on the cylinder's grip rail, trying to explain that it is impossible for the bottle to explode, that the pressure within forces the gas out of the nozzle where it ignites on contact with the air. "No, no, the flame cannot 'jump' into the bottle," he says. "All you have to do is step up and turn the gas off at the stopcock, simple as that." The chef to his immense credit is still there, eyes narrowed and suspicious, not wanting to trust this apparently crazy man. Petrus has made a tactical retreat to the safety of the kitchen, his swagger now quite gone, his credibility with the waitress entirely lost.

Without warning, there is a sudden and immense explosion, a blinding flash of light followed by a boiling cloud of dirty-white, foul-smelling gas. A hullabaloo issues from the assembly and when the smoke clears there is no-one in sight except Alvis, stretched his full and unconscious length upon the ground, frightened into an full faint, and Paul, still coolly standing at the flaming gas bottle, the entirely unmarked, unaffected gas bottle. I stand rooted to the spot, mouth agape. I hear the sound of a slamming door, the back door to the kitchen, as several of the more timid Namas make good their escape. Charles is as confounded as anyone, blinking behind his glasses.

"*Ek het myself amper gekak,*" (I nearly shat myself), he eventually says. "You training people, you're going to lose me half my staff if you go on like this. *Jislaaik!*"

Alvis opens his eyes and as memory suddenly returns he rises unsteadily to his feet and shuffles off in a slow semi-circle, his left leg apparently not yet in coordination with his brain.

"What the hell?" I ask Paul, still shaken.

"The chlorine/brake fluid mix," he says. "That was a good one, hey? I always make it a slow burner so that it takes ages to explode. I think they understand now *exactly* the dangers of fire."

16

HUBRIS

Lloyd, you're driving straight back to Windhoek tomorrow, aren't you?" asked Chris. "Can you give Dan a ride? It would save me the journey."

The ice in our tumblers of Jack Daniels makes music and the *mopane* wood coals throw out a fierce radiant heat. Desert Rhino Camp, deep in the Palmwag area of north-western Namibia, is one of the most peaceful places on earth. I'm sad that I'm about to leave: visits with my friend Chris, the manager, are always lively, filled with ardent political debate, songs and poetry, and epic guiding stories from the past. Plans for the future, too. These desert nights fill my heart like few others can. But I need to make the eight-hour trek back to the capital to get Chris's friend Dan and my Magalena Corporation guiding colleague Gregg to the airport in time.

"It'll cost you, Chris. Another bottle of Jack and more of your company," I tell him.

Serenaded by the wailing of the little desert jackals, we leave just before dawn in our white Toyota Hilux, the standard *bakkie* for the tough conditions of the rocky north-west, driving east into a rising orange sun.

"*Dankie ou maat* (thanks old friend). Don't do anything silly!" says Chris as I aim the truck for town.

It's a standard farewell. Drive safely. Take care. Don't do anything silly. We all say it reflexively. But today I should have taken more heed.

Dan is from Pretoria, a man of the city, but keen on the bush. He's now my responsibility. He sits in the back seat, content. It's been a great holiday in excellent company, and he's relaxed, dozing. Gregg in the front passenger seat is an experienced guide and an old colleague from Mombo Camp in the Okavango Delta. He's very keen on photography, and has all his equipment with him, as always, nestled in a grey plastic Pelican case. We crest a rise, the *bakkie* hammering noisily over the basalt stones. On the undulating boulder-strewn plain below us, and about 100 metres left of the road, stands an elephant. An old bull, feeding peacefully on the sparse desert grasses, his back to us, ears flapping lazily. He's relaxed. We stop to admire him: there's plenty of time to get to Windhoek.

"Come on, let's take a closer look," I invite Dan.

"*Ja*, I'll get some pictures, nice low angle stuff. Gorgeous light," says Gregg.

"I can see him from here," says Dan doubtfully.

"No, I mean, let's walk *down* there," I say.

"I can see him from here," said Dan, more firmly.

But Gregg is already out of the car, his camera unpacked and in hand, and on the move. I walk behind him down the slope, Dan following slowly, his hand shielding his eyes from the glare. We stay on the road, remaining at a respectful distance from the elephant, which continues to feed without concern. It doesn't even look up, just continues to pluck at wiry vegetation, fanning itself, one hind leg crossed comically over the other.

The sun is backlighting the elephant, his massive bulk dark in contrast with the red basalt and the overlying blanket of blonde grass and scrubby bush. There are no significant trees anywhere. In fact, there is no cover at all. But Gregg and I have been guiding safaris in the presence of large animals for years, and we know how to read their behaviour. All the signs here are positive: a relaxed old bull accustomed to passing traffic, paying no attention to us. He starts to tug at some wild melon vines, twisting the tendrils around his trunk and drawing the spiky green fruit closer to him, as if he is eating spaghetti. We proceed confidently, and reach the bottom of the valley, still walking on the road. The vehicle is 150 metres away now, but Gregg and I aren't at all concerned: this Jumbo is a grand and ancient bull, perfectly content to have us there. We watch, talking quietly, and Dan is quite calm now, enjoying being on foot in the presence of this old guardian of the bush. Gregg is down on one knee, shooting into the rising sun, trying for the kind of photo that makes the front cover of *National Geographic.*

Suddenly a sound like a wet hessian sack being beaten breaks the perfect morning stillness. The bull has spun around in a cloud of ochre dust and slapped his ears against his head, and is facing us now with his head lifted. A length of vine hangs incongruously from one stubby tusk.

"Don't worry Dan. He's just toying with us. No problem," I tell him.

But then the bull drops his head and flattens his ears against his skull and comes at us. From all of 100 metres away he charges! I'm quite surprised at this and I laugh a little. Gregg just keeps shooting pictures, the big bull shedding dust from his wrinkled hide as he bears down on us. But we've both seen this before, many times. It's a mock charge. I grab Dan's wrist.

"It's cool, Dan. He's just kidding. They do this," I tell him.

Dan, to his immense credit, stands dead still, although his eyes are wide, giving away his fear. He's breathing hard, but he says nothing.

And sure enough, the elephant suddenly stops with a clatter of stones about fifty metres off, and regards us with an uplifted head, sighting us down his great white teeth. I thought so: just a friendly warning. Gregg turns and looks up at me, and produces a large grin.

"He was false feeding, the bugger, and he was watching us the whole time," he laughs.

They're wily and wise these old bulls; they know all the tricks.

And apparently they have a sense of humour too! The elephant has been pulling up vegetation the whole time but not actually putting anything into his mouth. He's lured us down to his level under false pretences, and he's had some fun with us. Fair enough, but we have called his bluff, stood our ground, and now the game is over. It's time to leave. But as far as Gregg is concerned, the picture opportunity has just became even better: the elephant is closer now, easily filling the frame of Gregg's Canon 300 millimetre lens, and this is too good to miss. We stay.

This turns out to be a mistake.

The elephant comes again! This time I *do* get a fright. To run is suicidal: there's nowhere to hide on this barren plain and if our nerve breaks now, if one of us runs, this bull will focus on him and hunt him down. There is only one thing you can do in these circumstances: you stand your ground. We stand, and he thunders down upon us, his tail stiff and horizontal to the ground. The game has now advanced to second phase. My grip on Dan's wrist tightens, and although he tugs just a little, he stands. Good man: you never know how a person is going to react to fear. Natural instinct usually takes over and fear roots them to the spot, which is exactly what is required, because the attacking animal will back off if you show apparent defiance. But sometimes a person runs, and that can have tragic consequences.

The elephant stops about thirty metres away this time, rams his ears out hard, extends his trunk, and trumpets. It's a shrill blast of warning and the echo across the rocky red dawn is appallingly loud. Now I am scared. This is not going according to plan, and for the first time I realise that we are in trouble. I'm amazed that this has happened at all, and I'm feeling a simultaneous mixture of embarrassment and fear. My mind is racing, looking for options. Options? None, except to stand, or, if the big fellow will allow it, at best to beat a very, very cautious retreat.

Chris' farewell warning echoes yet in my mind. "Don't do anything silly, guys." Sorry, Chris.

Cautiously, we begin to shuffle sideways up the road. The elephant glares at us, grants us a few metres, and I start to hope that we might emerge from this with some dignity after all.

Then the bull charges. Again.

"Stand still!" bellows Gregg, loud and aggressive and authoritative.

This is a warning to us as well as a challenge to the elephant. To my astonishment, I see Gregg drop back into a crouch and aim his camera once more at the oncoming bull. I know from past experience that Gregg likes it a bit edgy, but he is being marvelously cool this morning. The elephant is absolutely huge, blocking out that fresh young sun, immense and dark and utterly terrifying. At six metres, at the point when I think that we are done for, the bull comes to a shuddering stop, looming over us with outstretched ears, his awesome piggy eyes furious and cherry-red, and perfectly deliberately kicks hard into the gravel with his right foot, showering us in light grit and dust. I hear the sand patter against the lens of Greg's camera, and a small gasp (but that's all) from Dan. The great bull trumpets again, a shattering scream that dies slowly in the desert air.

We stand. There is nothing else we can do. In the quiet as we wait for the elephant to decide what will happen next, in that concentrated stillness, I hear my heart hammering like rolling thunder high up in my throat, and I realize that I haven't exhaled for ages. We stand, and wait.

The bull measures us up, as if deciding whether our over-confidence has been adequately punished. Possibly, somewhere in the recesses of that mind, he recognises and respects our courage too. Perhaps. But whatever he's thinking, he's taking his time about it. For a very, very long minute, he holds us there, his trunk curled, his ears hard and wide and ragged on the edges, his enormous, intimidating bulk blocking out the light, with his tusks, smooth and yellowed, the ends chipped, held high. I notice small details: his wiry eyelashes, the horny toenails, the rancid smell of him. It is a cool morning, but I am bathed in sweat.

The elephant turns. Suddenly, as if he has made his mind up, he spins about with a strange, deep rumble, and walks quickly away. We have been reprieved. But we will still have to play this carefully.

"Easy boys. Slowly," I try to say.

My mouth is parched, and the words come out as a subdued croak. We inch away, but the bull stops walking. Oh, come on! But it seems that we have indeed earned our release, because although he watches us sideways from about twenty metres away, he lets us go. The joke, apparently, is on us.

We gain the sanctuary of the Toyota, slide in, and sit without talking for a short while. Our shirts are wet. The elephant is still down there, still watching, and now he walks onto the road itself, just where we had been standing, eyeing us coolly. A further challenge? Gregg and I look at each other. No more risky stuff today. I start the *bakkie* and back over the rise, getting out of the elephant's sight. We'll have to find a different route. There's no need to say a thing: a hard lesson had been learned. Dan leans forward between the front seats and speaks:

"Um, so, guys, is that, like, *normal?* Jeez, you *okes* (guys) are chilled. I never realized you just let them run up to you like that! God, that was exciting. I can't wait to tell Chris!"

17

WHICH YOU HAVE
ALREADY CONSUMED

Did she just say that we're eating *pumpkin shit* tonight? Malcolm, what kind of safari have you brought us on here?" asks Al loudly.

I look enquiringly at the waitress, Anna. She's local. She's grown up in an extremely remote village among the wildlife in the red rocky "torra" mountains of Damaraland, Namibia. In her short life, she has chased cheetahs away from the oblivious flocks of goats by day and she's banged pots and pans together at night to scare marauding elephants from the precious family water reservoir. She has walked as a matter of course the ten kilometres to school, barefoot, when there was no money for shoes. It has been a hard and simple existence with short horizons of expectation.

She's seventeen now, and her father has told her that she has had enough schooling for a girl. However, an opportunity has arisen. Wilderness Safaris has a joint venture eco-lodge over in the next valley, and it wants to give more people from the community the chance to learn new skills in tourism. Already the Damaraland Camp is managed entirely by members of the conservancy, but there is a need for a new waitress, with on-the-job training and a good starting wage that will make all the difference to a struggling family. It's been a dry year, again, and the cattle are showing their bones. It's a terrifying prospect for Anna, but she has friends and family among the staff at camp. They managed, so why shouldn't she? She's faced Black Rhinos, lions and Spotted Hyenas on foot. She shared her life on a daily basis with scorpions, the heat and the roiling east wind when it comes with violent intent in the deep of winter. It's not these things that scare her.

It's the tourists. They are strange people who talk and laugh and move in strange ways, and spend their time looking at her world through their cameras.

"Pumpkin shit, Malcolm? Damn!" says Al again.

Al is pretty deaf and his hearing aid is whining like an angry bee. Malcolm and I are leading a group of Magalena Corporation clients on a Namibia-wide safari and we're at dinner at 'Dam Camp', as the manager, Maggie, calls it. Maggie has been around for years, starting as a young waitress herself and moving steadily up the ladder. She's a treasure: experienced, patient, friendly and prone to sudden outbursts of song that amuse the guests as they lounge before the wide open view, peacefully reading their holiday novels and catching up their travel journals.

"Probably not," says Malcolm, recovering from a small choking fit. He's in danger of spilling his Cabernet.

Maggie, sitting with us for dinner, is in fits of laughter, wiping tears from behind her glasses. She remembers well. She too was chosen, a young girl whose first language was Damara-Nama, but equally fluent in Afrikaans. English, though, came slowly: nobody spoke it at home. The tourists come from all over the world, speaking in their indecipherable accents, asking for complicated foods without wheat and sugar and salt. They always seem to be intolerant to some kind of food. Things she'd never heard of before, like gluten and MSG. She's used to it now, though. The Americans want their glass chock full of ice, the French like to smoke at table if they can, the South Africans drink brandy and Coke until the early hours. The Germans ask for "ham" when they mean bacon, the Swiss can be a bit indifferent about the local cheeses, while the Norwegians sound like they are singing when they talk. The Japanese want to cook their own rice, and the Italians seem to spend their time happily yelling at each other. It's sometimes a nerve-wracking business serving this polyglot community of holidaymakers. And it's hard to get their attention: half of them are updating their Facebook profiles or reviewing their photos on their iPads and the rest are waving their hands in the air as they talk, making new friends, swapping game sightings and travel stories. It's a tough task for a nervous young village girl.

"Sorry for interruption," says Anna in a thin and reedy voice as the main meal is about to be served.

Everyone keeps talking. It will never do. Anna is standing behind me at the head of the table. It's her very first time announcing dinner, and she has been practicing all afternoon. This is a big moment for her and she is anxious to do well. She wants to impress Maggie: word will filter through to the village and she mustn't let the family down. Maggie, being an old hand, raps her knife sharply against a wine glass, and immediately a hush falls over the assembly. She smiles encouragingly at Anna and gestures with her hand. Come on now girl, she's saying, you can do it.

"Um, sorry for interruption," announces Anna again in a firm, high, hurried tone. "My name is Anna. Welcome to Damaraland Camp, the best camp in Africa. I would like to announce the dinner for tonight. The starter it will be ... "

A horrified look overtakes her. The bread rolls and hot soup have already been delivered to table and most of the guests have already laid down their spoons, the soup long ago eaten. The guests look at her expectantly. Anna swallows nervously but she recovers swiftly.

"Um, the starter," – and a shy smile plays across her lips – "which you have already consumed, it was ... butternut soup!"

Wow, great English Anna, where did you pluck *that* from? I think to myself. There is a bit of chuckling and several of the guests make gracious comments about how it is the best soup they have had on this on safari.

"Thank you. And for the main, it will be, um ... " she continues hesitantly.

Oh God, which meat is it? she thinks. There are so many types and these guests eat it in so many ways. Rare, medium, well done. It's so *complicated*, and there are so many foreign menu items to memorise. Back at the village we just boil up some goat or roast it over the coals. I'm never going to remember ...

But then it comes to her.

"Golden blue chicken, with pumpkin shit!" she squeaks triumphantly.

The guests look up, startled. Eh? Anna's accent is tricky to decipher, but did she say ... ?

Malcolm is spluttering over his wine and Maggie and I are convulsed. We're trying not to make Anna's discomfort any worse, but the dinner guests are perplexed and several of them are giggling loudly. Maggie regains control of herself, and rises.

"Excuse me everybody," she says with a smile. "Anna is new here. She's a little nervous, and her *French* is not quite perfect yet. The main course tonight is, of course, *cordon-bleu* chicken with roasted pumpkin seeds. Carry on please, Anna."

The poor girl is shaking, but she's game. These people eat such strange food, she thinks. And so much.

"Yes," she resumes. "Thank you. I am Anna. Um, you will have also a sexy green salad (What does *that* mean? I think. Still, give the girl credit for ingenuity) and for the starch it will be ... "

She hesitates, the panic creeping back.

"Rice," whispers Maggie urgently as the diners chortle and exchange smiles.

"Lice!" shouts Anna in joy, knowing that she has only dessert to announce now and then this will all be over.

No-one wants to be unkind but this is too funny. Even Al has managed to hear this one and is repeating "Lice. Oh my God. Lice!" again and again. This time Malcolm *has* spilled his wine and he's taken to beating the table lightly with a breadroll. One guest leaves the table to recover, mopping at her eyes with a table napkin. When I look again

I find that Anna has fled, and I feel awful for her. But then, almost immediately and followed by Maggie, back she comes, her uniform neat and her name badge perfectly straight. They've been outside the dining tent, practicing. And brave young Anna is upright and ready to try again. And this time it is *she* that raps confidently on a wine glass. We respect her courage, and fall silent.

"Thank you. I hope you will enjoy your pumpkin shit and lice tonight. (Wow, talk about rising to the occasion! Good going, girl!) For the dessert, it will be ... chef's surprise!"

"No kidding!" shouts Al.

"Yes. Thank you. For your dessert, it will be ... (in a rush, the words tumbling over each other) cigarette pudding!"

At this there is an uproar. Anna looks stricken but Maggie, her mentor, steps in once again.

"Yes, folks, that one is also quite hard to pronounce. It is called Sticky Date Pudding," she explains, giggling a little.

She signals the other waitresses to start serving. But I'm watching Anna and she has been enveloped by a small scrum of colleagues, all laughing with her and saying "cigarette pudding and pumpkin shit. Oh Anna!" and swatting at her playfully with their serving cloths. She's going to be all right, is Anna, a credit to the camp and her family. She'll quickly learn to pronounce all these western dishes. I can see that she's going to be just fine.

"Well," says Malcolm, rising with a recharged glass and addressing our group. "This is going to be an interesting meal. Bon appétit, everyone!"

18

SPAT

All at once, my right cheek and ear are coated in a fine damp mist, and reflexively I jerk my head away. Rain? In the Namib desert? In winter? My mind accelerates from neutral to nimble, creating and rejecting explanations at blinding speed. The sky is a typical Namibia azure blue. There is not a wisp of cloud. So it isn't rain, then. Has a passing bird pooped on me? No, it's not a bird, either. Because in that same split-second I understand exactly why my cheek is suddenly wet. This is not good. I can see the culprit in my peripheral vision.

Zebra Snake. Once again, that old too-familiar sensation of dread overtakes me, and time stands still.

Its ugly, rounded ebony snout is mere centimetres from my head as I spin round to face it. The cobra is unbelievably frightening at this range. Its flared black hood makes it look immense, and the small eyes glitter darkly. It's perfectly motionless, lining me up with deadly intent and a fixed, focused gaze. With perfect clarity I see the arrangement of the scales across its flat head and the alternating bands of cream and white down the length of its body. It has slid about thirty centimetres out of its rock crevice towards me but there's another metre of its long zebra-banded coils still hidden in the crack.

In these frozen moments of perfect presence, there always seems to be an inordinate amount of time to think, and analyse. Does the venom attack the nervous system or the body tissues? Cytotoxic, I think. Yes, the tissues. They inject fast-acting venom into their prey, immobilising it quickly and causing necrosis, but to warn something off they can also accurately spit potent venom into their attacker's eyes, causing massive pain and even permanent blindness. It had the option of biting me right now but it didn't: it spat. So this is just a warning. But this standoff isn't over.

The cobra flicks its nasty little tongue at me, tasting the air. Western Barred Spitting Cobras, known in Namibia as Zebra Snakes, are chiefly nocturnal and don't like to be disturbed from their rest. They're also known to be irascible and are inclined to attack with little provocation. This little gorge is steep and narrow: there is no retreat. I start to slide my boot away, feeling for a solid surface. Very slowly, I shift position, placing my feet carefully without looking down, shuffling them among the leaf litter, searching for secure footing.

This would be a bad time to stumble. Move with certainty and calmness, I tell myself. I sway my body slowly away from the serpent. It follows, maintaining the distance between us. But there are limits as to how far it can go: it needs to maintain a purchase in its rocky niche. I know it could still squirt me again. Into my eyes, this time. Is there enough venom left to spit twice? Stop looking at it, fool! But I'm mesmerised, like Mowgli under the spell of Kaa in *The Jungle Book*. I can feel the venom tickling slightly as it trickles down my ear lobe. But now the cobra begins to withdraw, making an honourable retreat, pulling back into the diagonal crack where it was basking in the winter rays. You don't usually get a second chance with these snakes, I reflect. Even so, I urgently need to wash the venom from my face and out of my ear.

"Hey, what's up?"

It's Simon. I've forgotten about him. He's at the top of the gully. I murmur quietly up to him in what I hope will sound like an

SPAT

authoritative tone.

"Stop there Simon. Do not come down here, " I say firmly.

"What?"

He can't hear me properly. With deliberate, controlled calmness I speak again, somewhat louder this time. I'm still gradually edging away from the snake.

"Wait there Simon. Wait there."

"What's the problem?" he replies.

There's a rattle of pebbles and Simon comes barrelling clumsily down the defile, scattering twigs and landing with an awkward thump on the fragmented rocks next to me. This situation has just got all complicated again.

I had taken responsibility for Simon earlier today. My friend Braam has brought a small group of us up Nambia's highest mountain, the Brandberg massif, called Dâures, the Burning Mountain by the local Damaras. It is a lozenge-shaped plug of red volcanic granite that juts up out of the arid desert gravel and glows like fire with the rising of the sun. It is a wild place, once sacred to the bushmen – the San – who climbed this vast rock island-in-the-plain to smoke herbs, hallucinate and trance dance, so that they could enter a world of spirits with whom they communed. They painted what they learned upon the many smooth, rosy, rock canvases that this mountain offers. Their lives and visions are depicted through thousands of individual images that adorn the walls and roofs of their temporary cave shelters, in pigments of blue and red and white and black and grey.

Some of these paintings are of snakes. Big snakes, such as African Rock Pythons. And others, reared up, ready to strike. Zebra Snakes.

But there's almost no water up here on the Brandberg, certainly not at this time of the year. The paltry rains have already petered out, the pools and streams have dried up, the little seasonal cataracts have stopped flowing and the striped mountain frogs have long since sought sanctuary, aestivating for the winter beneath the broken coarse gravel of the highland plateau. If you want to walk up here in the footsteps of the Little People, the first people, you will probably have to carry every drop of water you'll need. Despite the desert winter,

125

it is hot during the day. The unforgiving sun bakes the granite outcrops, stressing the rock, and then the cold of night fractures off great slabs of it, sending them skittering down the cliffs like plates of shattering glass.

The Brandberg may be an unforgiving mountain but beauty surrounds you. Even now in June the *dubbeltjies* flourish in swathes of bright yellow flowers. Rock Hyraxes, small rabbit-like mountain mammals, populate low rock chambers, keeping a watchful eye for Black Eagles which come sweeping around the buttresses with frightening speed on nipped wings, the wind whispering in their feathers, graceful in their menacing intent, their flight something from a dream in its magnificence and control and awesome majesty. And in the dusty floors of the larger caves, in the powdery soil where once San left their footprints, we find the *spoor* of a female leopard, her neat pugmarks leading to a jumble of mountain rock and tangled Brandberg *Acacia* thicket.

Braam had given us an orientation and safety briefing at the start of the hike.

"It's all about water up here on the Brandberg," he tells us. "Fill your bottles before we leave the cars. There may be no water until we return here in three days, unless we find some by luck. You'll come to understand the value of water on this mountain. Sip it slowly."

He goes on. The Brandberg is utterly remote, he explains. In its narrow ravines, you are alone in this world. Several hikers have died up here, disorientated, exhausted, finally succumbing to thirst and despair. There is no mobile phone network available. If you are injured and cannot walk, you'll have to save yourself through logic and calmness and the sensible actions of your friends. You will not simply limp off this mountain. Your only chance is if a colleague walks far enough to find a signal and manages to call a chopper: even then the helicopter still has to find you among the watercourses and canyons of the Brandberg. And that will take twenty-four hours at best, so you would need to stay alive until then. Stay hydrated. You take this mountain lightly at your peril; it's a place of beauty and it can be a place of death. Oh! And there are snakes here. Pay careful attention.

Last night was an incredible experience. We slept in a cave on the top of the escarpment and the roof was emblazoned with the massive painting of a giraffe. As we looked towards the west at nightfall, Canopus cast its starry spectral light over the Atlantic Ocean, illuminating a bank of grey marine cloud as the echoing barks of a troop of black-pelted Namib baboons rang through the cliffs. It was humbling. To think that the artist himself, hundreds of years ago, would have experienced just this scene.

And despite his prediction, Braam found us water, too! He followed the evening flight of the Rock Pigeons and found a thin stream creeping down the rock, accumulating in a little pool, more than enough for all of us.

Today we were aiming to climb a high peak and left this morning in the cool dawn. There was no clear route across the disintegrated sliding scree but Braam nonetheless set a cracking pace up front, springing from rock to rock like the agile little *klipspringer* antelopes that make this mountain their home. I trailed along in the rear with Simon, a pleasant teenager, a bit out of his comfort zone up here. Yesterday he twisted an ankle when a small boulder rolled out from under him. It wasn't too bad, but painful enough to slow him down and I could see that he would struggle on this ascent. Sure enough, halfway up he slumped wearily in the half-shade of a flaking yellow *kobas* tree. I waited with him until Braam came scrambling back down to us, the plated rock chiming like gongs beneath his boots.

"You guys okay? It's hot, hey! The people up there are running a bit low on water."

"*Ja, china*, we'll be okay, but you guys need to go on. We'll slowly head back to the cave. Here, take the rest of my water; I'll drink when we get back to the stream. You'll need it more than me up there. We've got Simon's bottle," I'd said.

He'd hesitated. No-one should be without water on the Brandberg, but it wasn't that far back to the cave and its life-giving stream. He'd trusted my judgement and taken the bottle gratefully.

"Okay. Thanks," he said. "But please be careful."

We'd relinquished the shade and started back down, Simon trailing gingerly some way behind me, favouring his ankle. My mind was disengaged: I was just strolling along easily in the wilderness under a broad sky with the clear whistles of the Pale-winged Starlings providing agreeable background accompaniment. Before me lay a small ravine, a narrow gap cluttered with boulders and strangler-fig trees. I'd negotiated the maze and was almost through but found my way blocked by a car-sized rock, scored through with veins of quartz. A long diagonal crevice ran across its face. Leaning against it, my right arm against the rock, I had searched ahead for the way down.

And now it has started to rain. A spurt of liquid on my right cheek, and deep into my right ear. Eh?

Rain? Bird? No, it's ...

"Hey, what's up? What's the problem?" shouts Simon from the top of the gully.

And then he comes cannoning into the picture.

The Zebra Snake comes straight back out of its crevice. This time it's taking no prisoners. Simon is off balance from his slide, and focused on stopping his fall. Panicked, the snake lunges hard at him, loses its grip, and misses its strike. In a twisted knot of coils it tumbles from its crack, lands in an inelegant heap on the ground and goes racing away between the rocks in a blur of black and white stripes. It's had enough excitement for the day. Disaster has been averted; I've been lucky.

"What the hell was *that?* Was that a *snake?* Hey, what's that stuff on your face?" asks Simon, regaining his balance.

"Zebra Snake. Cobra venom ... pass me your water, please Simon," I say tightly.

The venom feels cool on my skin. I hope there are no open scratches on my face. I know that the venom needs to be injected through the fangs to enter the bloodstream, but still, it's unsettling. And it's penetrated deep into my right ear: can it get through the skin of the ear lining? I doubt it but even so, the faster I can wash it out the better. It's already been there a minute, at least.

"Simon, wash this off me, man, quickly!"

"Um, sorry, Lloyd, I've just drunk all my water. It's finished.

Actually, I was going to ask you if I could have some of yours. Oh! Oh, *ja*, you gave yours to Braam."

He looks stricken. A fatalistic calm descends upon me. When you've just nearly been bitten by a cobra, nothing else really bothers you. I tug at my scarf, begrimed by two days of accumulated sweat and desert dust, and wipe at the venom, hoping to get it all, being careful not to smear any of it into my eyes, nose, mouth. There's nothing I can do about the stuff in my ears. I sponge at it but not effectively. It'll have to wait for the water at the cave. That's a nervous hour of walking away. But I'll be all right.

It's all about water up here on the Brandberg.

Sue and me at Damaraland Camp, Namibia. (Photo: Bill & Barbara Bigelow)

Full frame with a lion at Mala Mala Game Reserve, South Africa, where I started my guiding career.

Young cheetah near Zibalianja Camp, Botswana. Sue and I managed this camp for two years.

Hippos can be cunning and dangerous, especially when you are in a dugout canoe, as we found out from a man called Isaac at Jao Camp, Botswana.

I love leading clients to Vumbura Camp in the heart of the Okavango Delta.
(Photo: Rick Mann)

You need to mind your manners with the old "Dagga Boy" buffalo bulls that rest at night under the walkways at Mombo Camp.

With a Mountain Gorilla in Bwindi Impenetrable National Park, Uganda.

Jake looked the great silver-back straight in the eye ... and spoke to him.

Cessna light aircraft are the mainstay of the safari industry for transfers of both tourists and freight. Reliable and hardy ... if on occasion a little bumpy in the air. (Photo: Norbert Grafe)

Crocs are cute when they're small, like this one near Xigera Camp in Botswana ... but they don't stay small for long.

In the Great Sand Sea of the Namib Desert. (Photo: Geoffrey Paul)

A young Himba girl in traditional dress of goatskins, and coated in butterfat and ochre.

Serra Cafema Camp, far northern Namibia, on the south bank of the Kunene river. A linear oasis that harbours hungry crocodiles.

Playing with Himba children near Serra Cafema. The Himba are nomadic pastoralists who thrive in this hostile environment. (Photo: Graham Springer)

Exploring the bleak Skeleton Coast with Wilderness Safaris. There's so much more here than meets the eye. (Photo: Norbert Grafe)

I have walked countless miles and slept at many camp fires with my old friend Chris Bakkes. (Photo: Norbert Grafe)

Old elephant bulls are usually relaxed ... but this particular one surprised me one morning near Desert Rhino Camp, Namibia.

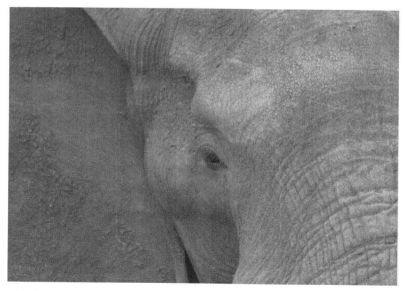

This close on foot is too close.

The glory of an Okavango sunset never grows old.

On game drive at Vumbura with Magalena guests. (Photo: Graham Springer)

Every guide should know how to open a bottle of bubbly with a machete.
Near Singita Sweni, Kruger National Park, with Magalena. (Photo: Graham Springer)

Bush camping with Wilderness Explorations in the Palmwag Concession, Namibia. (Photo: Norbert Grafe)

Walking in the Hoaraseb river, northern Namibia. Lions, elephants, rhinos and tribesmens' cattle frequent this seasonal water. (Photo: Norbert Grafe)

Into the wild, and loving it. (Photo: Norbert Grafe)

Toasting yet another great day in the wilderness. (Photo: Norbert Grafe)

Helicopter view over the Xigera Lagoon, part of the sparkling waters of the legendary Okavango Delta.

A grand old tusker in the Ngorongoro Crater, one of the iconic wildlife destinations of Africa.

A baby gorilla in the Volcanoes National Park, Rwanda. You only get one hour to sit with these wonderful primates.

Africa's dust on my boots and her warm breath in my lungs.

The Perfect Acacia – a classic umbrella thorn at Mombo in Botswana.

Sundowners: the traditional end to a day in the African bush.

PART II
EARLY ESCAPES

19

IN STITCHES

My youthful misadventures started way back with that horrible strutting red garden rooster.

The brute has treed me, and I'm trapped once more in the loquat tree.

I've always had a talent as a youth for getting into scrapes and effecting narrow escapes. It's the way I've grown up, barefoot and outdoors, ignoring the cuts, blood and bruises that accumulate as part of my daily adventures. There's no stifling mollycoddling from my parents, and legislated health and safety measures won't replace good old common sense for another generation, so life is always full of fantastic, unsupervised, misconceived adventures. Last year when I was four years old, I ascended to the top of a rickety old cupboard that my mother has expressly forbidden me to climb, and while I was up there I swallowed a glass marble that I was sucking at the time. Kids do funny things. I was saved from choking because in my panic I fell off the wobbling cupboard and hit the cement floor so hard that the marble was ejected, rattling against my teeth, then popping clean out of my mouth. I never told my mom about this close call: she would have been disappointed with me for disobeying her. And I feared the wooden spoon thrashing that I deserved.

It's a mystery to me that I have survived this long without suffering permanent damage. My wonderful mother deals with my minor injuries by vigorously brushing the wounds clean with a hard sponge and swabbing liberally with antiseptic Dettol; she is firmly of the opinion that accumulating dirt is a good way to build a healthy immune system. Speaking of that, I'm not sure if she knows that I have a curious fondness for eating mud clods and licking wet pavements. I'll bet she does, though: moms seem to know everything. So maybe my skin-scrapes and bruises are the least of her worries.

She's going to have to take *this* situation seriously though. I'm five, and I'm wounded yet again.

Last time the rooster trapped me in the tree I fell out of it as I tried to escape, and as I lay there winded, the arrogant bird lorded his victory over me; chuckling, eyeing me, with tilted head and wobbling comb. But this time I have a two-stage plan: I'll hurl a handful of the orange-yellow loquat fruits at him to distract his attention, then make a dash for the high garden fence, and try to balance above cockerel height all the way to the back veranda. It should work. It's better than sitting in the loquat tree all day.

But no! Here I am on the ground bleeding again, the red monster once more victorious. I didn't notice the long nail protruding from a gum pole in the fence, and it's pierced my left shin, gashing it to the bone as I leaped for safety. The flow of blood is terrifying. Even the red cockerel seems intimidated by the wailing I have set up, and as my resigned mother issues from the house, wiping her hands on her apron, to face the latest catastrophe, he's dodging away. Good thinking, rooster: no one messes with my mom.

She's rinsed out the hole in my leg and the bone gleams white within: this is going to mean stitches, which is terrifying. The last time I was transported to the Greytown village doctor, in floods of tears, to be sown up, the harassed man began his work with the dreadful curved needle too soon, even before the anaesthetic could really take effect, and the memory of that burns clear and bright. I'm shrieking even louder now and imploring my mom to "just put a plaster on it!" The red cockerel, now thoroughly alarmed and fearing retribution, has sought refuge on the roof of the pigeon loft.

I end up with three stitches but of course the accumulation of scars is a time-honoured childhood inevitability and the initial pain is quite easily compensated for by the administration of an ice-cream from the Rendezvous Tea-room on the way home. Furthermore, the fine white bandage will soon become the envy of all my little friends. Thus are local heroes made.

Fast-forward fourteen years, and it remains a great regret that I have never broken a limb severely enough to warrant a full-length plaster cast and a pair of those fine, tall wooden crutches. All I can boast thus far, apart from some cool scars, is a mere greenstick fracture and a simple arm sling from when I fell off my bicycle while doing "buck jumps". This gained me some limited respect at junior school but legendary status is ensured only by severe injury. Commonplace diseases like chicken pox and German measles count for nothing. *Everyone* gets those. I did manage to get tick-bite fever when I was about seven, though. The medication gave me nightmares: I was convinced that there were small green cobras living down the sides of the bed. That got my friends' attention all right. I'm still not sure they weren't real, but you have to trust your mom in these circumstances.

I came close to a proper fracture when I was ten, though. I slipped in an algae-infested drainage canal while chasing a homemade boat and landed with violent force on the back of my head. I set up the usual hullabaloo while my mother clucked in frustration at me as she shaved my head to gain access to the cut, but the net result was only another line of stitches. More resigned sighs from the Greytown doctor. He got to know me well.

On the other hand, the village doctor at Ixopo, where my grandparents have a small farm, has only met me once previously. A mad Dalmatian dog sank its canines into my right knee in a fit of playfulness (we cousins were playing leapfrog and the dog joined in, you can't blame it) resulting in a neat row of six stitches of which I was understandably proud. Given my track record, it's inevitable that the doctor and I should meet again. But I wasn't expecting it to be today.

Christmas Day. We teenaged siblings and cousins are old enough now to drink with our parents (although naturally we do most of our drinking secretly without them) and it has been a particularly memorable Yuletide feast with plenty of wine. Barefoot, bare-chested and not quite sober, we have repaired outside to kick the rugby ball around on the lawn. Tiring of this I have decided to display my gymnastic skills. Swinging upside down from a horizontal tree branch, a feat I have often previously achieved with success, the limb has suddenly snapped off just as I applied my full vertical (and upside down) weight to it. I have crashed two metres down, my head has struck a protruding root, and once again a river of blood has ensued. I'm sitting stunned on the ground while my brother and cousins point out that I might have been grievously hurt had I landed on anything but my head. Dazed and gory, once again I am in need of medical assistance. The village doctor has come to the phone having barely digested his own Christmas pudding and has graciously agreed to stitch me up, but only once he has amputated the mangled finger of a local farmer who has apparently entangled it in a grinding machine. What's that farmer doing, messing about with farm machinery on Christmas Day? (What am I doing, swinging about in trees?) Cousin Nils has placed a six-pack of beer on the car seat for me. He's encouraging me to partake liberally, reminding me that village doctoring tends to be less genteel than that which one might find in the clinics of the city. My head swaddled in a bloody towel, we drive to the village.

The doctor's not there yet so we cousins entertain ourselves with an impromptu game of beer-can skittles while the blood clots in my hair. He finally arrives, and it's obvious that he too has enjoyed a few lunchtime beverages. Scrubbing the wound energetically with a hard brush, he's quick to agree with Nils' helpful contribution that it's pointless looking too deeply into the head cut since he's unlikely to find anything of interest in there at all. Twelve stitches, another funny looking haircut and I'm done.

It's a grisly business, accumulating legendary scars!

20

CHOOSE A GOD
YOU TRUST

"Actually," says Ibrahim quietly in a conversational kind of way, "this is the *second* time that someone has saved my life like this."

What? I feel like letting him sink without trace. The sharks can have him. He shouldn't be allowed out alone, this man.

I met a hot little number, Samantha, on Second Beach yesterday: sixteen, bikini, bronzed, blonde ponytail, the whole thing going on. I'm in love. She claimed she didn't know how to body surf and I was happy to play along, teaching her, holding her up in the waves, being the expert. I finished my matriculation school-leaver exams a week ago: at last, twelve years of school was at an end. I'm starting university after this summer vacation but until then it's all fun and games down at the beach at Port St. Johns on the South African Wild Coast on a family holiday, relaxing after the stress of the finals and awaiting my results. Samantha is from somewhere in Johannesburg, and she seems quite keen on me.

Now, as I float in the sea with Ibrahim, I wonder where she

is. Did she make it? Second Beach has a reputation for fatal shark attacks. Apparently it's actually quite hard to get killed by a shark. I read somewhere that statistically there's a greater chance of dying of electrocution from a toaster toppling into your bath but I, for one, never make breakfast in the bathroom. There's a meat processing plant just north of here, up the coast where the Mzimvubu river discharges into the Indian Ocean, and the blood and animal waste that finds its way into the water attracts feeding sharks. Hyenas of the sea, those things. Bull Sharks can survive in salt water *and* in fresh water rivers. It seems a bit creepy to me, that. Almost unnatural.

"What do you mean? You nearly drowned once before?" I ask Ibrahim.

Ibrahim can't swim, it turns out. This guy shouldn't even be allowed in a *shower* unsupervised. He tells me that he was hanging in an inner tube on an inland dam somewhere once, missed his grip on the slick rubber, slipped through the hole, panicked and was fortuitously hauled out of the water limp and barely conscious by a passing ski boat. It hasn't stopped him playing in water, apparently. Either Ibrahim has a short memory or he doesn't learn. But I hold on to him.

The coast is a long way off now, a distant green line of bush getting further and further away. I've been watching it slide by for over an hour. Every now and then when a swell lifts us I think I can just make out tiny figures fishing from the rocks on the sea's edge, calm and blissfully unaware of our peril. Gosh, I hope Samantha made it back to the beach.

"Sir?"

Ibrahim has taken to calling me sir. He's in his mid-forties and I am eighteen, so it sounds strange to me. But in this situation I'm the boss. Overhead, gulls wheel by. I envy them. They'll be on shore in minutes. I'm trying not to think about Bull Sharks.

"Ibrahim?"

"Shall we pray, sir?"

It's always seemed hypocritical to me to ask a god for help only in emergencies. A bit late to be asking for favours, isn't it? That's like putting a plaster on a severed artery. I'm not going to start now. I roll my eyes a little: Ibrahim can't see me because I'm behind him with a firm grip on his swimming shorts. I've been holding him like this ever since he inadvertently tried to drown us all just after Samantha and I got to him as he floundered in the first line of breakers. He was panicking, sinking fast, and he swarmed all over me, trying to get up, striving for the light and the great good air. They taught us at school how to handle this. Once I'd fought my way out of his frantic grip I smacked him very hard across the face, which shocked him, then shot around behind him and grabbed his swimming costume, yanking it tight, crushing his testicles, holding him from behind. The irony is that at that point I could still stand, only just, although I could feel the rip tearing out past my legs on an ebbing tide. In a few seconds, though, we were in deep water and being carried out fast.

"Samantha," I'd yelled, "get back to the beach. Call the lifesaver. Go. Go!"

She'd looked pretty competent swimming away from me, surfing the waves, nice long strokes, neat little feet kicking hard. "She *does* know how to bodysurf after all, the little flirt!" I'd thought. "I hope I see her again."

"I don't really pray, Ibrahim. Do you?" I replied.

I've released the pressure on his privates now but I'm still behind him, holding him up easily in the salty water, talking to him over his shoulder, and now that we are out beyond the wave zone and there are no breakers crashing down on our heads, forcing us under, at last he has relaxed a bit. He trusts me. He has to: I'm all he's got. Well, me and his god.

"Yes sir, I do. Allah will save us, if it is his will. I will pray for us both. And for protection from the sharks."

Oh, so he's heard about those. Thanks for the reminder, Ibrahim. Well, who *hasn't* in these parts? The talk on the beach is that they've taken eight swimmers and surfers in the past five years. There are no shark nets here, too expensive for this small municipality to maintain, and research shows that they are virtually ineffective anyway. The sea is so shallow for such a long way out that it feels perfectly safe to wade and frolic and play but we're fooling ourselves: these Bull Sharks can easily swim into waist-deep water, it turns out, if they fancy a nibble on someone every now and then.

Ibrahim starts to intone in what I suppose is Arabic and I let him get on with it. I need him to be calm while I think. The immediate danger of drowning is over now that we have been washed through the backline but, sharks aside, all hell is going to break loose if we get thrown up on the littoral again. It's a rocky coastline and the jagged sandstone is covered in swathes of sharp-edged brown mussels: it's definitely going to hurt and it's probably going to be bloody. I haven't told Ibrahim this: I'm taking this one disaster at a time. The shoreline is littered with ship jetsam and old sea-weathered trees so I'm pretty sure that we will hit the coast at some point, but it's very unlikely that it's going to be on a forgiving white sandy beach. I think I have the strength to hold Ibrahim up for a while yet: it's not too strenuous keeping him afloat in a warm sea, so whether Allah intervenes or not, I'm making plans for the next phase.

Actually, there is something calming about having one's options narrowed in this way. Life becomes so simple. A strange kind of peace descends upon you: you control what you can, and leave the rest up to fate. Or God. There's no Twenty-Year-Career-Plan while you bob about at sea in shark territory. There's only now, and here.

I have always wanted to save someone's life. Always wondered how that felt, to give someone the opportunity to keep on living, when otherwise all their dreams, their hopes, their Holy Grails, would be snuffed out. And whether when the time came I would have the bottle to do it. My highest hope this morning was to come down to the beach, find Samantha, make some conversation (awkward, probably), and persuade her to go swimming with me. Maybe an ice-cream later. An Eskimo Pie with a lovely girl was going to be the highlight of the day. Not this.

I hope she made it. It's getting pretty lonely out here. She was swimming powerfully when I lost sight of her but with Second Beach you never know: it suddenly plunges away where the deep water begins, and there's a terrific backwash which is hard to escape from. So close and yet so far.

We're drifting steadily south and yes, I think the remote green hills *are* definitely getting closer. I can see a small crowd hurrying down the path, picking their way through the jumbled mass of shale and sandstone. Rescue party? Could be, but surely there's no way they can see us out here, two small dark heads bobbing in this vast balmy blue? If we're going to make it today, it's going to be down to me. Strangely enough, I am not very afraid; I feel calm. Fatalistic. I'm pretty sure I'll survive the landing though I know I'll be lacerated by the mussels. Of course, I've bled before. I'm not so sure how Ibrahim the non-swimmer is going to cope, though: we're going to re-enter the wave zone at some point, just before the horror of the mussels and the rock snarl begins, and he's really going to hate it. Maybe I *should* do a little praying!

"But who is your protector?" asks Ibrahim after a long pause.

He's so relaxed now that he's getting philosophical. An hour ago he was virtually dead, coughing up foam and thrashing his life away, and now he wants to discuss religion. I'm not in the mood.

Samantha had spotted him first. It was just like in the movies: both his arms thrown above his head, mouth open in a horrified, silent scream, eyes white and wide. We were with him in seconds, clasping his hands, our feet braced against the insistent, deadly tug of the current, feeling the sand washing from beneath us, knowing that we were losing this battle, and seeing the absolute certainty in this man's eyes that he was about to die. He went suddenly mute when I hit him and grabbed him by the gonads though, my other hand around his chest and cupping his chin, deliberately allowing us to float away from shore, out through the breakers. You can't fight the current. All you can do is slip out through the crashing waves, reach the calmer swells behind the backline, keep buoyant, stay calm, stay alive, and wait for a second chance. Pray if you think that helps.

"Go, Samantha, go!" I'd shouted desperately.

At least I have my answer now. *This* is what it feels like to save someone's life. The job's not done yet, but now I know that I can answer the call. I just did it without thinking, swam up to him and grabbed him. So far, so good. So now a new question arises: if

I actually had had time to consider whether to save Ibrahim's life, would I have done it then? What if I had time to weigh it all up, balancing the personal dangers against the immediate instinct to save his life? Would I have done it? I think so. I'm not sure. Every answer brings a new question.

"My protector? Ibrahim, today it is you!" I joke. "I'll do the swimming, you do the praying, let's see how that works out. Teamwork, hey?"

I'm half joking but he's not. He carries on praying. The restless ocean is unquestionably taking us in now: the rocks are getting closer and the smudge of land is materialising as a small red cliff, the spray of the broken waves at its base fountaining into the air.

Suddenly, a splash of white water, close at hand! My heart lurches. Shark? The movement is shielded by a rising swell and then there it is again. It's a ... person! A man swimming athletically, his tattooed arms churning, yellow fins thrashing at the sea. It's the lifesaver. He's swum a very long way to reach us. It's scarcely believable. The fact that he has even found us out here borders on a miracle. Useful things, miracles.

"Happy to see you *china*," I say to him. "Look Ibrahim, here's the lifesaver."

I'm flippant and relieved all at once. But it's funny, the lifesaver looks grumpy, even somewhat put out, as if we've inconvenienced him. Maybe he's exhausted? He doesn't say much. Still, it's nice to have some professional help and a weight lifts from my shoulders: now I can focus on saving myself. We're close to the shore now, about to re-enter the wave zone, and it's going to get tricky again. I release my grip on Ibrahim's swimming shorts, expecting the lifesaver to take over responsibility. Immediately, Ibrahim sinks like a stone.

"Hey! Grab him, man!" I shout. "What the hell?"

I can't figure the lifesaver out. He seems strangely disinterested. He's the one in the day-glo, high-visibility swimming outfit, the fins, with the golden tan and the muscles, the guy with the training ... but it's like I have gone and interrupted his day and he's not happy about it. I reckon this guy failed "Communication and customer service" at Lifesaver School. And now he's let Ibrahim go.

Ibrahim saves himself this time. He surfaces like a depth-charged submarine, comes high out of the water, kicking wildly, latches onto the lifesaver and proceeds to climb all over him. The lifesaver goes under in a maelstrom of limbs and bubbles but Ibrahim stays afloat. I've seen this before. An hour or two ago. How long have we been out here? I stroke over and take hold of his trunks again, from behind. Ibrahim is babbling incoherently, his fears re-asserting themselves, immediate death back on his mind. He's absolutely terrified.

"Cut it out! Ibrahim! Hey! Shut up!" I scream at him.

He flinches; he thinks I'm going to slap him again. He goes quiet immediately, and looks at me with frightened, disappointed eyes. He cannot believe I let him go, and he starts to shout again.

"You, you! *You* must help me!" he bellows.

He's not interested in muscle boy. I'm his guy. Seems like I'm still the rescue boss around here. The lifesaver bobs nearby, looking chastened. I look at him angrily as we tread water in the foam.

"I've got this, *china*," I tell him. "Hold Ibrahim by the costume. Just help me when we reach the rocks, okay?"

The lifesaver looks happy with this arrangement. He's still hardly said a word. It is a very strange and unexpected morning indeed. He grabs onto Ibrahim's swimming shorts.

"Did Samantha reach you?" I ask. "Is that how you knew about us out here?"

"Ja boet." ("yes, brother.")

Well good, that's a huge relief. I've been feeling responsible for her. People are concentrating now in small knots on the little cliff and I can see one of them has a flotation device attached to a yellow nylon rope, but right now it's superfluous: he can't get close enough to toss it to us. The mussel-ribbed rocks look forbidding, angular and threatening, the waves riding up in thick green walls against them, foaming through the shells, ripping back down in cascades of broken white water. We're going to bleed. The lifesaver is probably thinking the same thing and regretting having accepted this holiday job.

"Ibrahim," I say, "the waves are coming again. I've got you, okay? I will not let you go, I promise. But listen to me now. Are you listening?"

I'm shouting above the wind and crash of the sea, yelling into his ear with urgency and he knows that this is the end game. He nods. Good man. I feel a sudden warm affection for him: we're bonded in a dreadful situation and he trusts me. He has chosen to place his faith, and his life, in my hands.

"Listen to me the whole time, okay? The whole time. Do not look at the rocks. Do not look at the shore. Do not look at the people. Listen to *me*. I'll tell you what to do. When I say NOW, you hold your breath; you hold it until we come back up. Got it? Say yes. Say YES!" I shout.

"Okay, okay, yes," he says quietly.

The fear shows in his eyes and in his tight mouth but I know this is going to work. The first wave comes combing in. The lifesaver and I tighten our grip on Ibrahim's shorts. A green wall of malevolent water smashes down towards us.

"NOW!" I yell out.

The breaker smacks us on our heads and we go under, deep, but we're up in a trice, floating high. No problem. And then the second one. Under. Back up. Floating. They're getting bigger, driving us towards the rocks. Under again, longer each time. Ibrahim is magnificent, so brave, sucking air into ballooned cheeks, then spitting out water and gasping in breath again. He's pliable and limp. He's surrendered his fate to me. And Allah. But right now it is my skill and will to survive that counts. A fourth breaker comes creaming in, swamping us. We spin and somersault like three men in a giant washing machine but we hang on for all we're worth, arms twisting, legs flailing, and then up we come once more, Ibrahim's cheeks comically puffed out like blimps, and we breathe the welcome air. He has found courage that he never knew existed within him. We've only got a few seconds to take in air ("NOW Ibrahim, NOW!") and it's very hard to hold onto Ibrahim with one hand but we've got him ... and I can hear people shouting, and the guy with the buoyancy aid is right in front of us, and now we're at the rocks. We surface for the last time before we strike shore and I yell out once more in the brief interlude as we languish in the final trough:

"Look for the rope, Ibrahim!"

A massive comber lifts us, carries us, drops us on the limestone with numbing force, and we grab at anything we can, slipping on tongues of green algae, fighting for balance, for purchase, feeling the cut of the mussels on hands and feet, struggling against the receding water, trying to clamber up the rock before the next mean wave can rush in and claim us again and haul us back into the deep. And now helping hands are here: the yellow nylon rope and a brave soul, with barefeet and bikini. It's Samantha! Brave, foolish, silly girl. (I'm definitely in love!) She's amongst the bedlam of tangled limbs and white water, risking her life once again. In the chaos I fall and lose my grip on the floundering Ibrahim, but the lifeguard has him (this time) and he's hustling him to safety, passing him up to outstretched hands. The vengeful ocean releases us at last and Samantha and I clamber up the sandstone ledge, hauling ourselves up the rope to safety, and we sit there on a smooth rock, breathing hard. Blood seeps from my hands, from the soles of my feet, from a torn knee. Less blood than I had expected, actually.

The Wild Coast sun is hot but I'm shivering, goose pimples across my entire skin. Unexpectedly, I start to cry a little, tears of relief and salvation. Samantha puts her slim, cool arm around me. It feels delicious.

"Well done," she says simply.

I'm thrilled to hear her say it. Samantha is holding my hand and wiping blood away from a small wound using her finger. I'm Clark Kent. I'm Bruce Wayne. And Achilles, too, a vulnerable warrior.

I don't know where Ibrahim has got to. Some-one hands me a pair of plastic flip-flops and a beach towel. I can't talk properly: my tongue and lips feel salt-swollen and I'm mumbling with fatigue and cold. Why can't I feel the warming sun? Some guy is trying to give me something to drink: bizarrely, it's a beer. Castle Lager. Thanks but not right now, *china*.

"Hey, that was awesome *boet*," he says. "Good job. Lekker! I *checked* the whole thing."

We walk slowly back to Second Beach, and here's Ibrahim sitting cross-legged on a towel on the sand surrounded by his family. He looks better than I expect. A bit pinched and blue but not too cut up at all. His wife is berating him.

"Again! The second time! Again! Oh, Ibrahim. You are a stupid, *stupid* man."

She's beside herself, beating him energetically with a folded beach sarong, crying and laughing at the same time. Ibrahim is looking suitably sheepish. He points at me.

"This is the man. He is the one. And the girl," he says.

Ibrahim's wife rushes up and embraces me, crying, running her hands over my head, saying "thank you, thank you, thank you". I point at Samantha and she gets the same treatment: her hair is stroked as the woman whispers incantations over her. I don't know where the lifesaver is: probably back on his high beach chair, combing his hair, planning his next tattoo, cursing us for disturbing his tanning time, I suppose.

"I will ask Allah for his blessings upon you, sir. Ibrahim says you and he were praying for salvation," says Ibrahim's wife.

"Um, well, Ibrahim was praying. I was ... "

"It is good. It is right. Allah answers all prayers. He has returned you to us. It is written. To whom were you praying sir?" she asks.

"Well, I was just keeping my fingers crossed, really," I reply.

"It is important that you choose a god you can trust," she admonishes, shaking her head.

But I'm not talking about being saved from the sea. To do that, I swim. Actually, out there in the ocean, my fingers were crossed for Samantha. Samantha, and Eskimo Pie.

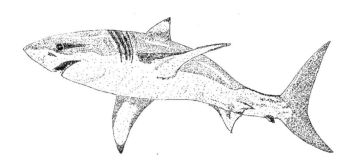

21

LESSONS FROM LUC

He did it. It was almost unbelievable. The guy helped *me* across the line. Luc ran the "Big C", the Comrades Marathon on heart alone. He had courage in abundance and the fortitude of a lion. He needed that. Because he harboured a dreadful secret.

My friendship with Luc had started some months before, on a Tuesday.

Someone jogs past me in the opposite direction. I'm on the long uphill section, Alexandra Road, trailing the front runners, pushing hard, but my watch is telling me that at this pace I still won't be running a personal best on my weekly time trial, Herman's Delight, this evening. I am wholly occupied by voluntary pain and ready excuses. Too humid, too much beer last night, I ran too far on Sunday and I'm paying for it now, too much to eat at lunch, too much of too much. Put some heart into it, Campo, I'm telling myself, but the central governor in my brain is saying "Chill man, there's always tomorrow. Take it easy! Lots of time before The Big C, it's still only March." But I'm training for my first Comrades, an annual road running race of eighty-nine kilometres from the coastal port of Durban to Pietermaritzburg, my home town, I'm nervous as hell about the challenge and I want to see the results of my training. Now.

"Where are you people all running to?" asks the guy who just went by the other way. A vaguely French accent. Intriguing.

He's obviously turned around and caught me up. Weird. Wow, he's *fast*.

"6.4 kay time trial every Tuesday. Called Herman's," I gasp.

He wants to chat but I'm at my limit and it's all I can do just to keep running, so he falls in annoyingly easily beside me and keeps pace until we cross the line. We regain our breath and introduce ourselves. He's called Luc and I like him immediately. He's light hearted and irreverent and refreshingly naïve about this running game. That makes me the expert and we end up drinking Castle Lager on the verandah of the Royal Hotel.

"I want to run this Comrades," he proclaims.

"Luc, it is on the 31st of May, my friend. I have been training for it since *last* year. You'll just injure yourself if you try it. Anyway, you have to run a qualifying standard marathon first," I counsel him.

"I'll run that one with you next weekend. Where is it? Durban?" he says without hesitation.

"*Ja*, but you can't just ... Jeez *china*, you'll be sorry, these things hurt!" I tell him.

"I'll be fine. Seriously. I'll really regret it if I don't try," he says, undaunted.

I came to discover that he lived without regrets. Later, I found out why.

So the following Sunday we run the Savages Marathon. Slowly. About halfway, as I predicted, Luc develops painful knees, slows to a shuffle and I jog on alone. But despite his injury he finishes in less than four and a half hours, within the qualifying time, and he enters Comrades, a scant eight weeks hence. He's a brave man.

Luc rapidly becomes a mentor to me, a hero, though I only came to recognize that in retrospect. He isn't a grey beard, but since I'm only twenty, and he is in his early thirties, he seems immeasurably more experienced and worldly than I am, a bit like an older brother who has travelled the world and returned with tales from the other side. He's a quantity surveyor who drives recklessly and lives his life at great speed.

Luc and I begin doing all our running together, and I love spending time with him. He's quite different to my university mates: older, foreign, a salaried man with some spare cash and a broader world view. Wise. Everything has to be an *event* for him. After we run, we always have to go out for beers and dinner afterwards, and he usually pays. We run the Elangeni half-marathon in Durban and I'm feeling exhausted after a hard effort, but he insists on going surf-swimming afterwards, then drinking cocktails in the sun at a beach bar. We drive up to the Arthur Cresswell, a fifty-four kilometre race between the small midland towns of Bergville and Ladysmith, and Luc insists on making a real weekend of it: camping and *braai-ing* the night before the race, a lunch after the race, then drinks in the pub. He's a life and soul kind of guy with boundless energy that I find inspiring. Luc gets things done.

One evening at his place we're drinking beer and listening to Michael Jackson's 'Thriller' and finally he tells me in his charming accented English exactly why he is so frenetic.

"I was born in Mauritius but I trained to be a QS in France. I was feeling not so good for a while so I go for a check-up and *merde*: lymphatic cancer! I'm too young to die, man, and I take the drugs and the chemo and I fight it, and I win. They give me the all-clear and I buy flowers for the entire nursing staff, and throw a party in the hospital ward. Champagne, caviar, the works. A big party: *magnifique!* Then I come to South Africa to start again. A second chance. A new life. New challenges."

He shows me a slew of plans and sketches and calculations for his dream project: to design a beach hotel in Mauritius. But now he's become so involved with his South African girlfriend, Christine, and his running, that I think that the hotel can be nothing but a pipe dream. We're running and drinking together five nights a week, and I feel I have made a friend for life.

And we duly run Comrades. As usual, we have an enormous pizza and probably too many beers in an Italian place the night before the race. Luc has both knees bandaged right from the start and they must be giving him hell, but he brushes off any sympathy. What are gammy knees compared to cancer? It's only pain, and pain is temporary. We progress nicely together as far as Pinetown, but then to my horror, in the melee of a sponging station near the bottom of Field's Hill, we lose contact. I run on without him, frustrated, and my day becomes progressively worse. Suffering from cramps and a sudden stomach ailment, I struggle to Pietermaritzburg, and finally reach the Jan Smuts Stadium, the end point, on the stroke of half past four, ten and a half hours after starting. My brother Gerald spots me as I struggle towards the home straight, and his voice penetrates the pain fog in my brain.

"Luc is just ahead of you!" he shouts.

I can hardly believe it. I crack on the pace, up and over the bank, and as I come down onto the field, with the finishing tunnel before me, I see him. More than anything, I want to finish this great race with my friend.

"Luc! Luc!" I scream.

Through the tumult of the crowd, he hears me. He turns, and stops, and stands there with a huge grin on his face, his arms wide open. It's been a desperately hard day, there is a mere 300 metres to go and here before me is my friend. I burst into tears and sag against him. He puts a protective arm around my shoulders.

"See, Lloyd, I told you we would run this thing. Now we finish together. Come," he says gently.

I'm drained in every sense, exhausted to the core, but Luc is so strong. We walk over the line together. Medals are draped around our necks, and it is finally over.

Over in more than one sense.

Because suddenly Luc is gone. This man who has taught me so much, who has demonstrated to me what the face of courage looks like, who has virtually carried me over the Comrades finishing line to help me achieve a life's dream, is gone. He's moved out of his rented flat without leaving a forwarding address, without warning or a word of goodbye, and he's disappeared. I'm devastated, bereft even, and

I'm feeling betrayed somehow that he has dismissed our friendship in this way. It makes me angry and confused: I feel abandoned. One day I bump into Christine.

"It's not personal, Lloyd. Luc has some unfinished business in Mauritius. Something else he wants to achieve before ... just something else he needs to do," she explains.

Perspective comes rushing in. The Comrades Marathon, so all-important to me, was only one challenge in his life, not the only challenge. I'd failed to recognize that. Luc has just inadvertently taught me yet another life lesson.

I continue to run Herman's, I even run Comrades again the following year, and I get used to not hearing Luc's cool accent on the balcony of the Royal Hotel every Tuesday evening. But it's not the same. I miss him.

One morning my friend Francois, another running colleague and a friend at university, bumps into me in the lecture hall. There's something odd in his voice.

"Luc's in town. I saw him. You should look him up," he says in a strangely hesitant voice.

What? I'm shocked, and incredulous. Why hasn't Luc got hold of me? Piqued, I choose not to try to find him.

A week later I walk into a restaurant in town. The place is full, buzzing with conversation. I spot Christine, sitting at a corner table with some shrunken guy wearing a peaked cap. It's Luc. He is decrepit, bald, and dying. I go cold. The cancer is back. How has this happened in only two years? How has this unwelcome evil taken residence in this vital being again? This man ran *Comrades* for God's sake, eighty-nine kilometres of blood, sweat and tears, this brave and essential man. Long ago he vanquished this enemy. Surely by now Luc has earned immortality?

Realisation floods through me. The cancer never really left. Luc never told me the whole truth. I am overawed, and I find that I am unequipped to deal with this moment. Fear settles upon me. Luc is leaving again, this time for good. I abruptly retreat before Luc and Christine can see me, before I am forced to face mortality, both Luc's and mine. My fear, and my failure to confront it will be my own unwelcome secret.

Why can't we just go for a run right now, like we used to? I stand for a while in the carpark, crying. For Luc? Or for me?

I won't go to his funeral. I won't let go of a hero. I don't yet know how to suffer loss. Some lessons you just have to learn by yourself.

22

NIGHT FIGHT

I didn't pick this fight. I'm desperately thirsty, and all I want is to get home in one piece, but Candidate Officer du Plessis is trying to get us all killed again. This time it's with his spearmint toothpaste.

Our platoon lieutenant, Chaplin, is making du Plessis bury the whole tube. Deep. Du Plessis is on his knees, digging contritely with his *pikstel* in the deep Owamboland sand while the rest of the patrol glares at him. Idiot. We're not *allowed* to brush our teeth for the entire operation. For twenty days and nights. Chaplin says the 'terrs' (terrorists) can smell the toothpaste from a mile away. We've got to try to blend in. We're so filthy that it shouldn't be too much of a problem. Well, except for bloody du Plessis and his fragrant minty breath. I could wring his grimy neck.

And we're thirsty. Very thirsty. I know this is the South African Defence Force and I never expected the army to be a cakewalk, but seriously, I thought the intention was to produce hard, fit soldiers who are battle ready. But our company commander, Captain Smit, the most miserable and vindictive man I have ever encountered, is cowed by the Regimental Commander, and is desperately keen to make a good impression on him. So we're out on patrol with everything the manual says we need for conventional warfare: rifle grenades, raincoats (it won't rain until November), cooking accoutrements, spare radio batteries that weigh a ton, extra uniform that we won't wear (they'll just become as foul as the ones we're in), *aapjasse* for the cool nights, far too many belts of light machine-gun ammunition, a seven-day supply of ratpacks and the worst-designed boots I've ever laced on. Back at Infantry School, our home regiment where we have done most of our basic training for this Junior Leader course, they make us run the Two Comma Four in those boots too. It's a weekly fitness test where we're supposed to run 2.4 kilometres in full battle kit as fast as we can. I'm a marathon runner in Foxtrot, the sports platoon, so I find this fairly easy, but half of us have shin-splints as a result of the impact under the heavy load.

When we walked the week-long *vasbyt* march three months ago in the wet and misty Swartberg mountains to test our physical and mental limits, we carried even more than this, and lots of trainees had to be evacuated because their feet packed up. It was the boots. I took a lot of strain with my feet but I made it all the way back to base after six awful days of bitter cold, driving rain and relentless badgering from Platoon Corporal Hanigan. Afterwards, horrifyingly, the soles of both my feet peeled clean away and I was on light duty for weeks afterwards, limping around in flip-flops. The blisters formed deep below the soles from the slow repetitive pressure, and the puss jetted out in an impressive and frightening thick yellow fountain when the medic drilled through the skin. How is an army supposed to march to battle and then fight in these stupid boots? They polish up beautifully for parade but out here on patrol they are useless. So we're walking for nearly three weeks in enemy territory, in southern Angola, with far too much kit, almost no water, lugging around mortar pipes and rifle grenades and entrenching tools, the sun beating down on us, and wearing rubbish footwear.

But that's the Army for you.

My question is, what is du Plessis thinking, carrying toothpaste and a brush? Even toothpaste weighs a few grams and all we want to do, all we think about, apart from finding water, is how to get rid of weight. Everything weighs *something*. I don't know, maybe he was just brought up that way. Old habits. You have to brush your teeth every day. Actually, no, du Plessis, you don't, not out here under the eyes of the enemy, not if it means we're going to get shot.

The guy's a nightmare, a real risk to our safety. Last night he nearly shot Corporal Hanigan! I could understand if he had actually *aimed* at him – Hanigan's one of those terribly *paraat* non-commissioned officers, deeply immersed in the army culture of intimidation, and a real bully – but this was yet another accident. Not surprisingly, Lieutenant Chaplin completely lost it with du Plessis, swearing at him inventively in several languages. He's promised to place him on orders when we get back to base. I hope the Lieutenant follows through: du Plessis has got to go. Admittedly, the whole situation is distracting: dehydration, bad footwear and uneasy sleep make a soldier jumpy. But still.

What happened was that sometime after midnight our lying-up position was compromised and we had to leave our shallow trenches and move to a new temporary base. I wasn't on perimeter guard when it happened, but it seems an old Owambo man had come wobbling down the sandy track on his bicycle, drunk as a lord, singing to himself, and he stopped for a piss right where we were lying in potential ambush. He would have peed right on one of the guys, so the rifleman jumped up out of the darkness and grabbed him. We had to move immediately and we took the poor old man with us, his eyes rolling in terror in the darkness, his bicycle hidden back there under some bushes. We let him go this morning of course, and no harm came to him, but the whole situation has escalated now because while we were moving in the darkness du Plessis committed the worst offence you can: he discharged his R4 rifle by mistake. You can imagine the pandemonium: soldiers hitting the deck everywhere, thinking we were under attack, nobody knowing what the hell was going on. The bullet went into the ground right next to Corporal Hanigan's right ankle. Hanigan turned pale even under all the camouflage cream he was wearing, and he just stood there in the moonlight, his mouth opening and closing a few times. It was nice to see him scared actually: a bit of schadenfreude going on there, I guess. No physical harm was done but the noise of the shot was shockingly loud in the stillness of night and I was blinded by the sudden light of the muzzle flash for a bit. I think the old Owambo man thought we were about to shoot him because he started to wail and we had to restrain him. Talk about being compromised: now every PB for kilometres around knows exactly where we are. So we've just had to keep humping our packs for hours to get out of the danger zone. Platoon two, Foxtrot Company are tired, grumpy and frustrated. Candidate Officer du Plessis is definitely going to get kicked off the Junior Leader course now: toothpaste is one thing but pulling off a shot is sacrilege. He's wasted eight months of hard training and now he's going to end up as a post office *tiffy* or something; an anonymous soldier with no rank, sorting mail back at HQ. We'll all be glad to see him go.

My task is to walk right behind the Lieutenant and keep count of paces. Owamboland is a flat and sandy floodplain that traverses northern South West Africa (which the locals call Namibia) and southern Angola. We have rudimentary maps but without any real landmarks on them they aren't much use. To navigate we walk in straight lines on a Mills compass bearing, counting the number of paces we take. The Lieutenant tested everyone and it turns out that I'm the one who walks with the most consistent pace and speed. It's obvious why Chaplin didn't choose du Plessis! After we cover 1600 paces I have to tell the Lieutenant, and he marks the map: one straight-line kilometre walked. It's surprisingly accurate, actually. The problem is that I have to really concentrate all the time, but I can't help daydreaming about fresh water. Water, and my girlfriend, Sue. I haven't seen her in months, and I miss her. Her letters are in my pack and I re-read them every day. They represent something fresh and innocent, untainted, so far removed from the terrible realities of this war I have been forced into.

We started this patrol south of the Cutline, the international border, with five litres each, but there's only been one fresh water re-supply since, and it is very hot. We're encouraged to drink only at night after we've set up our temporary base. Lieutenant Chaplin says we'll just sweat it all out if we drink during the day. I know better than this: I did a huge amount of mountain walking and marathon running before I was conscripted, and it's definitely much better to sip lightly all day. But I know why he says it: water discipline. If we simply drink whenever we like we'll drink too much, so to control that he halts the patrol every hour and we rest and take a small controlled swallow in the scanty shade of the *mopane* trees while the annoying little bees drive us crazy as they try to extract moisture from our eyes and nose and mouth. Captain Smit has forbidden us from asking the local villagers for water. I think he believes that since they are the enemy they might poison us. But *they* need to drink from their wells too. In any case, we're invaders on their land and they have hidden their wells. It's clever what they do: they remove the wooden T-pieces and winding structures that are normally embedded in the soft sand above the hole, put down planks and cover them with a thick layer of sand. By the time the goats have crossed over a few times you'll never find it. It doesn't help to ask the PB's: they hate us and just sit there with downcast eyes, sullen and silent, un-cooperative. I don't blame them: the Captain chanced across a well recently and dropped a hand grenade down it as an act of retribution. Evil bastard. These wells are deep, sometimes fifty metres, dug over generations, handed down from father to son, and represent the life-blood of the community. There are no rivers here: this is the only water until the summer rains come and fill up the *omurambas*, the shallow pans in which they grow their *mahango*, pumpkins and other crops.

So we're reduced to sieving the filthy water from the troughs where the cattle and goats drink. It's green and there is shit floating in it. We're desperate. We try to filter the gunge out using bandages from our first aid kits, then passing it through a clean pair of socks. We boil it, we put water purifying tablets in it, we mix it in plastic tubes from the ratpacks and make juice with it ... but still it tastes like shit. I had a bad spell of vomiting yesterday but I think I'm okay now.

I'm supposed to be counting paces, but my mind drifts inevitably towards water. It doesn't really matter though. The count is so automatic now that I do it pretty much without thinking, even at night when I walk to the toilet pit. A few missed paces here and there make no odds. Chaplin seems happy and we appear to be on route. But I keep envisioning a litre of ice-cold milk: right now, that would be the greatest gift anyone could give me. I promise, when I get back to the States, which is what we call civvy street, South Africa, I will buy a small bar fridge reserved only for drinks and keep it permanently stocked with milk. I swear it. I'll drink milk whenever I want.

The captain arrived on the back of a *buffel*, one of those V-shaped mine-protected vehicles, a couple of days ago. He's too fat to walk anywhere, really. It was quite a dog-show, him trying to locate us based on where he thought we were. The Lieutenant radioed our coordinates to him and we could hear the vehicle grinding through the bush towards us so we took cover. The Lieutenant doesn't like him either. At the last minute we threw smoke grenades, yellow ones to indicate that we were friendlies, and stood up on all sides of the *buffel*, pointing our weapons at him. He nearly soiled himself. His eyes were bulging and he couldn't talk for a minute but he couldn't do anything about his embarrassment: after all, it was done by the book. The driver gave us our rat packs while Smit was getting a situation report from Chaplin, but when he saw us filling our two-litre water bottles from the hull tank he nearly had an apoplexy, screaming at the troops to cease and desist, threatening disciplinary measures. It's the water in the hull that serves to buffer the force of a mine blast. I don't think he was scared of hitting a mine really, there aren't that many away from the main roads; he was just taking revenge for being made to look incompetent.

I spotted an old Russian-made mortar bomb this morning, just lying there dormant in the sand. It's rusted and the fins are bent, and it must have been there for years. I showed it to the Lieutenant and he mentioned it when he radioed in his daily sit-rep. Now the Captain wants us to go back and find it, and I will have to carry it in my pack all the way back to base. Extra weight. Potentially *explosive* extra weight! Stupid, stupid, stupid: I shouldn't have said anything. Never volunteer, keep remembering that, Candidate Officer Camp, I remind myself.

And Smit will ask for it when we get back, too. That's what he's like.

Our orders are to scour all the villages we come across and arrest any males between the ages of fifteen and forty-five. It's really difficult to guess their ages, and of course there's no way they'll tell us. In any case, word must have got out because the only people we are finding in the villages are women, infants and very old men. The military rationale for this is that the younger men are potential enemy recruits but all the healthy ones are at war already. They are long gone, training in Angola or Zambia, and infiltrating back into South West Africa during the rains, attacking SADF bases and infrastructure by night, mining the roads, then fading away before retaliation can arrive. The villagers provide succour and sanctuary to the 'terrs' at night and report on our movements so that we can be ambushed in our temporary bases, we're told. We're also told that we're winning this war, and we *are* if you use body count as a measure. But that's what the Americans did in Vietnam too, and they ended up leaving the country to the communists. That's what's going to happen in this war too. Fine by me. It's *their* country.

I pay attention to the international news on the rare occasions that I can get it. They say that our South African politicians are meeting with SWAPO, the South West Africa People's Organisation, the political wing of the majority people of this country, to put an end to this insanity. I hope that's true. I just want to survive my time up here on the Border. Walking pointless patrols like this is shortening my odds of that. When three jets flew high overhead this afternoon, heading straight into South West, I pointed them out to the Lieutenant. Chaplin is PF, permanent force, a career soldier, a good man, and he can separate propaganda from reality.

"MIGs," he said. "Russian-made fighter jets. Cuban pilots."

"So we've lost the aerial battle already?" I asked.

"*Ja*," he said, "our own fighters, the Mirages, are old and outclassed, they're being shot out of the sky. We'll lose the ground war too eventually, that's the way these things always go."

I wonder why he's here. He's different to most of the PF officers: he treats us like we are intelligent people and he knows we can't be fooled by the propaganda forever. He's pretty phlegmatic about it, doesn't seem at all upset that we're going to have to leave South West Africa and Angola. I guess he's looking forward to a cushy number in a base somewhere back in South Africa. He's got a wife and kids back home. Maybe not, though; maybe he's already planning to join a war in middle Africa, there's always one going on somewhere. Ex-SADF officers are highly sought after up there. Who knows? Good luck to him.

Tonight will be the sixteenth consecutive night I have slept in a foxhole. Four more to go. I don't mind lying on the ground at all though: the sand is cool and deep and comforting after the heat of the day, and actually I sleep quite well. I take my boots off at night. I just can't sleep with them on. It feels wrong, and my feet need to air. On *vasbyt* I didn't air them and maybe that's why the bottom of my feet fell off. If Chaplin knew he'd freak out: it's totally against protocol but I'm pretty fatalistic about it all. If we're attacked, I'm not going to be running anywhere, anyway. The safest place will be right here in my foxhole surrounded by other soldiers who know their job, maintain their arcs of fire and trust their training. I can pull an R4 trigger or fire off a Claymore mine just as easily barefoot as in combat boots. I hope bloody du Plessis isn't next to me if we're attacked, though. Mind you, I could just shoot him myself. It would be safer for all of us.

About three weeks ago when we were back at base a platoon from Echo Company came in from a similar foot patrol to this one. We Foxtrot guys were all relaxing in the bar, having our ration of two beers a day, chatting and listening to the Housemartins' "Caravan of Love" blaring discordantly through the cheap loudspeakers. I was thinking how bizarre it was that such a beautiful ballad could be playing in a place such as this when in they trooped, badly in need of a drink. It was disgusting; they hadn't washed for twenty days, their uniform browns were smeared and oily, their beards matted, their faces gaunt … and they stank. I could smell them from twenty metres. I went to talk to Lieutenant Davey, their commanding officer, and it was hard to concentrate; he smelled so awful it brought tears to my eyes.

"The great unwashed, the great unshaved, the very terribly behaved," I said to him, recoiling.

"You'll be like this too after your twenty days," he said, laughing. And we are. We're stinking, but alive. For the first few days I noticed it, but I can't smell myself at all anymore so I guess we've done what Chaplin wanted: we've blended in. Our faces and arms are so dark now from sunburn, camouflage cream, sweat and dirt that we look like the locals. I don't even need a notebook anymore. When the Lieutenant wants me to work out a distance based on my pace count, I just take a small twig and scratch the numbers on my trouser leg, through the grime, doing the calculations. Some of the guys draw pornographic cartoons on their grubby forearms. They look like reverse tattoos. One I saw was of Captain Smit, being rogered by an Owambo goat.

But I've just got to hang on. Lug this heavy pack full of unnecessary equipment for four more days, drink my cow-besmirched water and make sure that I stay awake when on night watch. Because we're all going on leave after this patrol, flying all the way back to South Africa like civvies in the Safair 737 from Grootfontein Air Base, for two weeks of bliss. I need to get away from the Army for a bit: it's stultifying. I need some different conversations, home-cooked food, cool water, and milk whenever I want it. They'll ask me at home about the Border and the Army and do they treat you well and how's the food and all that but it'll be the same answer as always: "*ja*, it's fine, yes, I've made good friends, no, everything's okay." They don't understand what it's like and I don't want them to worry.

My brother has already done his two years of military service. He was in tanks. I'd rather be out in the open *veld* than in a "tommy-boiler". (That's what the Germans called the British tanks in the war. Imagine being caught in a SADF Oliphant tank when a missile arrives in the cockpit.) But the point is that he knows about the military, he's done all this already, and he survived fine. He just smiles at me. "Your turn, *boet*," he's saying. And it *is* fine. It's an interesting period of my life, which will pass, like everything does. It seems impossible now, but I'll be forgetting the details of this involuntary adventure in a few years. I'll be forgetting the names of comrades, brothers in arms, upon whom my life now depends. That's the Army. That's life.

But right now I've got to hang on. I need to be careful. And I'll take luck wherever it favours me.

Because a funny thing happened just before we went on this patrol, the night Echo Company and Lieutenant Davey came in. Just after Echo had showered and shaved and shampooed in the shower trucks, just two short minutes of hot water per person, and sat down to their first proper meal in almost three weeks, all hell broke loose. Those guys from Echo were still wired from twenty days of relentless, sublimated fear, and when the first rocket-propelled grenade came into camp and exploded, they leopard-crawled for cover like there was no tomorrow. Which considering the circumstances, there might not have been.

We Foxtrot men were all still just standing there shocked with our *dixies* in our hands, dumbfounded, but the Echo boys were mobile, under the tables, behind the bar, legging it for the sand bag emplacements, and Lieutenant Davey was screaming commands: "On me, on me!" They didn't even have their weapons with them and I'm glad they didn't, who knows what they might have done, firing randomly into the night sky. Or at us.

There's a standard procedure for night attacks on base, though, and it was amazing to see how our training kicked in. The camp lights were doused, our mortars started coughing immediately, throwing up illumination rounds, and the troops on the outer defences added some thousand-foot parachute flares. In seconds the cleared ground in front of our small camp was lit up like a Christmas tree and our perimeter light machine-guns and a slew of standard-issue R4's opened up on the treeline, spraying the *mopanes* down with 5.56 millimetre lead. You could see the leaves being chopped from the branches, raining in green confetti to the ground, and the LMG tracers streaking out into the darkness. We all have pre-arranged places to go to in the event of sudden attack; I don't even remember running to my defence position, on a mound next to the huge black rubber bladder full of diesel in the centre of the camp, but by the time I got there I had my R4 in my hands and my whole platoon was in position, facing outwards, ready to defend the camp fuel supply. A second enemy RPG came in; you could hear the "crump" of the rocket igniting on launch from the distant trees. The firing went on for about a minute and then a commanding officer shouted "cease-fire" and it suddenly went still. The 'terrs' had given us a fright, then run like hell. Standard procedure for guerrilla warfare.

Total silence. Eerie silence. Everyone listening, alert, perfectly present. Just the sound of breathing.

There was a small fire burning over at the supply HQ where the first RPG had detonated near a tent, setting fire to some boxes and blankets. No-one had been injured. But what about the second one? I didn't remember an impact explosion. It's hard to be sure in the heat of battle.

I leaned back against the fuel bladder in relief. That could have been a *lot* worse. My whole body was alive, pins and needles all over my skin. Something heavy rolled off the bladder and landed with a gentle thump on the soft sand next to me. I looked down.

It was the second rocket grenade. A dud. It had landed right behind me on the fuel bag without going off.

That was three weeks ago. We're nearly back to base now. I have an old mortar bomb in my pack and bloody du Plessis has been trying his best to get us all killed. Just another twenty klicks of walking. I need to keep it together, man. I'm thirsty and I just want to get home.

23

FEAR OF FLIGHT

The rope is jammed.

It's stuck way above us in a cleft of rock, and without it there is no hope of escape from this mountain. We look at each other in horror. It has been a very gruelling day ... and it just got worse.

Orion has already started to hunt in the broad southern sky, his great bow pointed at Taurus, and his silver-eyed dog, Canis, is following as always at his heel. Among the high jumble of weathered rock, in the gloaming, my friends and I consider our plight. Our last remaining bottle of precious drinking water is mysteriously yellowed and foul, un-potable. We must have used a filthy bottle. We are exhausted, beaten up by the weather, by disappointment, by hunger and thirst. A ghostly blue moon is starting to cast long eerie mountain shadows over the desert plain below. The plain of sanctuary. We are running out of time. It's all gone wrong.

"Can you do it, *china*?" they ask me.

The plan to fly our paragliders off Spitzkoppe, an imposing red granite pinnacle and the highest free-standing peak in Namibia, has turned out to be fantastically misconceived. We knew it might be, but the three of us feel bulletproof and have a youthful disregard for consequence. It was worth a try, and here we are. It's a week before Christmas in the Namib desert and it is very, very hot. Mike and I have backpacked our gliders to the peak, and Arnulf has carried most of the climbing ropes and gear. It's a tougher climb than we expected and it has gone on all day, the merciless sun beating down upon our backs and heads, reflecting into our faces off the crystalline rock. I'm wearing a pair of borrowed *velskoene*, smooth soled and totally inappropriate for climbing. It's tough up here but we like it that way. Negotiating the claustrophobic cracks and chimneys is sweaty, cramped work, but it pales in comparison to the exposed final few pitches of coarse granite where the world drops away below your feet and where you have to trust the sinuous rope to hold you if make a false move. Somehow, in the footsteps of those hardy early Germans who forced a route up this forbidding tower a century before, we have found our way up and over the top section, and here we are at last, tethered to the summit cairn, shading our eyes in the harsh light.

But there is not a hope of taking off from this tiny rock plateau. Not in these winds. We started our climb at dawn with the sinking of the giant constellation of Scorpius, but the bulky gliders have hindered our progress. We've gone off-route twice on the way up, and now it is too late in the day to fly. Arnulf is watching Mike and me with trepidation; he's less foolhardy than the two of us and I don't think that he fancies a solo descent. Or picking up the pieces. *Our* pieces. But to take-off is not even an option. The wind is gusting hard and though we're roped together, we're struggling to stay upright. Far, far below we can see the smudge of Arnulf's yellow *bakkie* parked in the shade of a giant dome of rock, and the tiny, stick-like figure of our friend Frans, a non-climber, pottering about at camp.

"You get old pilots and you get bold pilots, but you never get old, bold pilots," cautions Arnulf.

Though we are reluctant to admit it, we know that he's right. Sanity prevails. We scribble our names in the summit book, place it back in its rusted tin beneath the flat plates of eroded granite that form the summit cairn, snap some pictures of each other – gaunt half-bearded mountain warriors in heroic poses – and start to abseil off the mountain. It's late, already way past two, and the mid-summer heat is unrelenting. The earth is a gulley-riven mirage shivering far below. Down we go.

The abseil anchor points (who placed these ring bolts, and how long ago?) look unreliable. We have no choice but to use them. To gain time, in some places we do some risky down-climbing without bothering to use the ropes and safety gear. Our hands and fingers are tender, abraded by the textured rock. Here and there we find scraps of shade and crowd into it but the wicked sun is asking questions of us today, and it's a higher-grade test. The descent is tricky and takes hours. We snatch a few handfuls of dry peanuts, and Mike extracts our last bottle of water from his pack: it's murky, and it smells bad. How has this happened? There's no time to wonder and little point.

We urgently need to drink. We need to get off this mountain. Our morale is still good, though: after all, this is what we signed up for, this type of adventure. But now the light has begun to fade and at the bottom of a dark and smooth-walled chimney, as I try to pull the rope through a ring-bolt, it somehow sticks fast. I lean my forehead against the grainy rock in frustration. There can be no further descent from here without this rope. For us to go down, I will first have to go back up. Earlier in the day, I was the one who led the summit pitches. I was the one who went off the top first, and who had to up-climb the rope at one stage when after the rope's full fifty metre length, I still had not encountered a good belay point. Mike and Arnulf look at me.

"Can you do it, *china*?"

One of them will go if necessary, but they're hoping I will. I gather my courage. I climb, towards Orion.

Much later, the little night birds already free-wheeling in a purple sky, we stumble out of the confusion of tumbled boulders and sharp-edged scree and onto the sanctuary of the desert plain. A fire is burning strong and homely from our camp in the dark shadows of the whaleback rock. Frans is there, waiting, anxious for news: he has been watching but no paragliders have blossomed in the azure sky that day. But now he has heard us coming, and the tea is brewing. Bless him. No tea ever tasted so good.

This friendship has been forged in a cauldron.

"Boys, that was epic," I say. "But I'm *done* with this mountain."

24

FEAR OF FALLING

The rope jerks twice. It's time.

It feels like things are about to go horribly wrong. I used to *love* this sort of thing. Hanging about on exposed cliff faces with hundreds of metres of absolutely nothing below me.

But right now, alone, cleaved to the rock, surrounded by unlimited open space, it is absolutely awful. I'm scared and I want to get off. It's a particular kind of fear that invades my guts, this fear of falling. If I do, my life will depend on a thin rope attached to a bolt placed by persons unknown. It is a very long way down, but down is where I most decidedly want to go. Slowly. Surely. Down.

I climbed Spitzkoppe ages ago with my friends Mike and Arnulf, but it's my brother Gerald who is the real climber in the family, the one with the talent and the need to scale tricky peaks and crumbling faces. At one time I showed some potential, scrambling about at our local crag on weekend jaunts with the Natal University Mountain Club, but then road running began to consume my spare time, and I abandoned the ropes for the road. I prefer roads these days. They're mostly flat.

And yet I've always wanted to be back up here. It's a magnificent mountain and it has always called me.

And so here we are, Gerald and me, on the ropes, sixteen years after my first ascent of this rock spire. Sixteen years, in fact, since I last climbed at all. That first time Mike and I lugged paragliders to the summit, but we sensibly chickened out in the gusting winds, and carried them disappointedly back down again. Memories of that climb remain seared in my brain: the harshness of the coarse granite on my fingers and palms, the intense reflected heat of the rock, the acrid smell of the *dassie* urine which streaked the cliff white in places where these rabbit-sized rodents had gathered to warm themselves on sunny mornings. But it is the desperation of having no drinking water that I recall most vividly. It was the heat and thirst and creeping darkness that scared me then, not the exposure. I'm older now.

Now, fear is a close acquaintance. It has settled on me like someone you feel obliged to invite for tea and who ends up staying for dinner. But watching Gerald climb, I see that he is at peace, magnificent on the mountain: he effortlessly embraces it. I fight and smear my way up its rocky flank in old running shoes, sweating and grunting in wide-eyed effort like a hard-ridden white-lathered horse, struggling with the mountain and wishing only for the summit, whereas my brother smoothly spiders his way upwards, assessing the face, confident and calm and composed, enjoying the journey. Now and then he stops, leans out over the abyss and, using one hand, takes a photograph of the shimmering plain far below.

I think back to that first climb. I had huge confidence in my athleticism and strength, then. I had no doubt that we would get it done. My climbing technique has deteriorated since, and now I just feel scared. But this is a choice ... it's tough, and we like it this way.

Gerald consults the route guide book, threads the rope through an old ring bolt, and tosses it over a small cliff to a ledge below which allows horizontal access to the top section of the climb. He cheerfully announces that since we have only two ropes instead of the recommended three, and will need both in the abseil off the summit, we cannot leave this rope behind for a retreat in the event that we fail to climb the final pitches.

"This is the point of no return," he says, grinning.

He's loving it. I'm glad he's in charge: his mettle is encouraging. I swallow, and we climb on.

Propelled by the potential embarrassment of failure, I claw my way up the vertical face, lunging for small handholds and inelegantly wedging myself into cracks.

"Hey, stop using your knees, brother. Bad form!" Gerald says, laughing at my poor style.

And yet, eventually, blessedly, scratched and bleeding, I am on top. It wasn't this hard last time. Was it? Time is balm to the mind. I peer over the edge. An indistinct pale blur in the shade of a stunted desert tree: Gerald's car. His wife Alison and their kids, tiny at this distance, relax at the campsite. I long to be down there, at the destination instead of on the journey. But I'm mindful that I chose this. I wanted to do something significant with my brother.

More than a decade on from that first ascent, our names are still in the summit book: Arnulf, Mike, Lloyd. Did we really hope to paraglide off this pinnacle? I sit very still and enter my name again (Gerald can't be bothered, so I write for him: we measure achievement by different degrees, apparently.) I do not like it up here; I feel threatened and exposed and unwelcome. Gerald, casually strolling around the summit, takes more photos and then prepares to descend. I survey the ropes and surreptitiously check my anchor point. I'm trying not to show that I am spooked by this.

What is loneliness? Loneliness is when the person you are depending upon disappears over the edge, you know he can never climb back up again, you cannot see him at all and the only contact you have with him is a taut, doubled rope, a brotherly umbilical cord. And a knot joining those ropes that looks decidedly iffy if you don't know enough about climbing. The wind is howling, the old, cold June wind that cuts like a cruel, blunt sabre across the desert and smashes into your mind and soul – and I feel lonely.

At last (after far too long; what's *happening* down there?), the signal comes. Two quick jerks on the rope, and the knot crams up against the ring of the bolt. I clip on rapidly and am away. Out of there! Looking down, down the length of the binary line that links us, I see Gerald hanging from the face. Hanging from the *vertical* face! I'm expecting, I think I remember from last time, a nice safe 'tea and scones' ledge. But no: there's just the unforgiving slab plunging down and away to oblivion, and an untroubled figure contentedly lolling about in his climbing harness, taking pictures. And now I remember. This is the bit where I had to climb *up* the rope last time. My mind has been saving me from this. I slide down the rope, the abseil plate friction-hot in my hand, and finish up level with Gerald but ten metres away from him. Another unwelcome surprise.

"Just pendulum over, *boet*, and clip on," he laughs. "I'll grab you when you get close enough. No man, *swing*, you have to really swing."

On my third attempt I get close enough to take hold of his outstretched hand and I hook on to the bolts. Gerald secures the bottom end of the ropes to our anchor point and pulls them through the ring high above us: fifty metres of rope plummet past us and dangle below. I don't want to hang around on this hostile red rock, and he knows it.

"You go first, brother," he invites me, smiling at my haste.

I abseil down, this time to a nice wide platform. Indignant *dassies*, their rest disturbed, reluctantly make way for me, creeping into shadowy crevices. Two jerks on the rope says "your turn". Gerald descends casually, stopping occasionally to admire the view. I close my eyes while I wait for him, and compose myself. I'm tired and thirsty, but the certainty of the rope and the sanctuary of this broad ledge has reassured me. The ground is closer. Then a sudden dark thought occurs and I check my backpack for water, the memory of that revolting foul potion of last time very clear. But this time a bottle of beautiful clear liquid remains. I drink thirstily and think of a different day on this mountain.

In the evening of that wintry day, as the wind-spiraled dust devils hurl themselves towards Scorpius rising, my brother and I carry our burdens of gear off that rock and out onto the welcoming plain. Our hands are raw, my knees and elbows bloodied. I throw the ruined and tattered wastes of my shoes away.

What is relief? Relief is when you make it back down to the pleasure of level ground after some part of your brain that you have deliberately tried to ignore all day thinks you might not. It's having climbed hard, above your ability, and made it. Not to the top but to the bottom.

We walk back to camp. Alison has the kettle on the flames and only once before has tea tasted better.

Climbing Spitzkoppe, emerging from it, may be the finest thing I have ever done with Gerald. The satisfaction of the achievement is hard to describe: it feels very good indeed.

We are brothers, forged in the cauldron.

"Gerald, that was epic. Now I'm *truly* done with this mountain," I say.

25

ZOBRA

"I will take you. It is many days. My name, it is Zobra," the old man said.

Being utterly lost is the scariest thing in the world. We know what Zobra is really saying to us: foolish young white men playing around in the wilderness; without me, you would have perished. You're damned lucky you found me.

Actually, we don't *have* many days left but we respectfully, willingly follow in his smooth wake for liquid kilometre after liquid kilometre, days without end, hungry as lions.

Just getting the two boats to the start of the adventure was a challenge in itself. The bright yellow, two-man, Indian-style canoe that Arnulf and I bought has maxed my credit card out but that's a challenge to face once we get home again. *If* we get home, the way things are going.

Mike had collared me some months before in the staffroom of Glenwood High School in Durban, where we were both teachers. The winter holidays were fast approaching. Two weeks of free time.

We had very little money to spend, sure, but that had never before stopped any of our adventures. It wasn't going to stop us now.

"Let's paddle the length of the Okavango Delta in Botswana. It's 250 kilometres from Shakawe village to Maun, the end point of the greatest inland delta in the world. Arnulf and Stu are already in," Mike had said with characteristic enthusiasm.

Old university friends getting together in uncharted Africa. It was an easy decision. And in our usual style, too: winging it, with limited planning, driven by the concept and without much consideration for the dangers, much less the details. We'd employ our usual tactic. Take it as it comes and make a plan when we need to. It was a typically outrageous idea and one we'd never heard of being done before. Hundreds of kilometres of unmapped waterways, floating papyrus islands, flooded grass plains, wild animals. How hard could it be?

So one day in July the four of us, accompanied by Arnulf's girlfriend Pat, rope the canoes onto the roof of Arnulf's yellow *bakkie* and set off for the Botswana border armed with some rudimentary topographical maps and very little else. Stu is supposed to have arranged the food but his catering skills evidently lean towards the ascetic. The maps show only a frying-pan shaped splash of blue among very wide-spread brown contour lines – clearly, this land is featureless and flat – but we are possessed of a naïve confidence, and that makes all the difference. We have a mere fortnight to drive nearly 2000 kilometres to the launch point at Shakawe, right at the top of the Delta's 'panhandle', paddle the 250 kilometres to Maun, the sleepy little donkey-ridden village where Pat will wait for us, and then drive all the way back to Durban. We estimate we'll have at least ten days on the water: hard paddling, certainly, but it should be sufficient.

As with most of our adventures, things get tricky on day one. At Martin's Drift, the border crossing into Botswana, the immigration official insists that we need a permit for the boats, only obtainable in the capital, Gaborone, several hundred kilometres south.

"T.A.B.," we say in wry frustration. ("That's Africa, Baby.") Arnulf and Pat gamely head for Gabs while Mike, Stu and I start hitchhiking towards Maun, just for the fun of it. I scribble "hitchhiking" under "mode of travel" on the immigration form. The laconic official's attention is aroused.

"What is this," he demands, "this 'hitchhiking'?" I demonstrate, holding my thumb out and simulating waving down a car with my other hand.

"Aah, *footing* it!" he says, noting my backpack and correcting my entry with a leaky black ballpoint pen before waving us through.

Arnulf and Pat finally catch up to the three of us the next evening as we sit disconsolate and dusty at the roadside near Gweta village, still en-route for Maun and only an hour or so short of our destination. There has been a dearth of passing vehicles. It turns out that the boat licensing actually needs to be done in Maun after all, not Gaborone, and we spend the next few days in frustrating limbo, being shuffled between government departments, the Police, Water Affairs, and the Department of Wildlife, registering the canoes for the Okavango and watching the time tick by. Furthermore, it turns out that we won't be able to use Arnulf's *bakkie* to transport our boats to Shakawe because the road is atrocious, rutted and sandy, suitable only for four-wheel-drive vehicles. A chance conversation in the Duck Inn, a watering hole for locals, procures the four of us and our boats a lift on the back of a builder's sand lorry that's heading north for Shakawe. We load up at dawn the next day. Finally, the adventure is underway.

Late in the afternoon, scorched by the sun and desiccated by a pernicious dry wind, we are deposited without ceremony by the roadside. We drag the laden craft a short distance to the river. Pied Kingfishers hover and dive, a Monitor Lizard splashes noisily into the water. We're talking animatedly. Our excitement is palpable. This is it! We have only eight days left to reach Maun. It's going to be tight: we all have jobs to get back to. And in the back of our minds lingers a story some hoary old-timer at the Duck Inn told us about a Japanese guy who tried this same stunt, became lost, and was eventually discovered wandering demented in the Swamp. We've avoided discussing it: it won't happen to us.

The plan is simple: paddle downstream in fast-flowing water until we reach Maun, sleeping on the islands by night to avoid lions, and fishing for nice fat bream to feed ourselves as we go. We have some rice, some tea, a little sugar and a large jar of peanut butter, plus a few packets of Provita wheat crackers. And there is plenty of water. You can just reach down into the crystalline Okavango and drink to your heart's content. It's been difficult getting these boats onto the water, yet here we are. We've faced our challenges. What now could possibly go wrong?

The stream is swift and southerly, powering along between high walls of tall *Phragmites* reeds, and we're feeling pleased with ourselves. That evening Mike catches a large bream, and we pull over to an island for the night, build a fire, brew tea and fry the fish. The pan sizzles, the tea is satisfying and the fire is warm; that night we settle in to sleep, mosquito nets over our heads, content in our company.

"Maun in a few days, boys," I say just before the sound of contented snoring overtakes our little campsite.

The embers glow under an immense southern sky. All is well.

By lunch the next day, though, we are in a quandary. We're already about sixty kilometres downstream, and we're not lost as such – we can point out our approximate position on the map – but the Okavango river has suddenly, dramatically, slowed and split into dozens of leads and a myriad floating papyrus islands. There is no obvious main route. We've hoped that a major channel would be evident. The cartographer has drawn fanciful solid-blue lines on the map that look like big rivers but down at water level it is impossible to figure out which one to take. The rushing flow wants to commit us to a direction, but once we make that decision we will be swept along, possibly to a deadend. Then, unable to paddle back upstream, we may end up having to sleep in our cramped little boats, awaiting a rescue that never comes. After all, no one knows where we are. We cling to the papyrus on the channel fringe and debate. Where is the evidence that people pass this way? Even a knot of bent grass would be a comfort. Sobering reality hits hard, and for the first time I begin to feel a tiny tendril of fear creep into my guts. I'm giving nothing away though. I hope.

"Boys," says Arnulf, "this is hopeless. We need to get to Seronga village. I don't know how far away it is but I'm sure we can do it from here. We just cannot go down this route. It *has* to be Seronga. We've got to find someone there who will show us the way to Maun."

He's right. The enormity of what we have undertaken settles upon us. Without debate, we start paddling east by dead reckoning while we still can. The side-channel we choose is narrow and winding and choked with water lilies but the going is fairly easy, and our concern is lifted occasionally by the sight of Red Lechwes, water-adapted antelopes, bounding in herds through the inundated plains, throwing up diamond sprays of broken water behind them as they splash away.

"Smoke!" shouts Stu suddenly. "Hey, guys, look, there's smoke over there!"

He is pointing urgently. Never underestimate luck as a life strategy. A village appears far, far sooner than we have expected, tucked in among a grove of Mangosteen trees, a circle of small houses constructed of branches, mud and tin sheets, the smoke from several domestic fires curling lazily up through the foliage. We draw our boats up alongside a long wooden *makoro*, a local dugout canoe, hauled up on the bank. A forked *ngashi* stick, used to propel the boat, is lying within, and a small cast-iron cooking pot and other simple possessions nestle in the prow: grey blankets, a worn jacket, a pair of shoes without laces, a sack of *mealie* meal, some fishing nets. Two skinny dogs spot us first and come bristling down to the beach in a frenzy of barking. Intruders! A small boy wearing a dirty red Liverpool F.C. football shirt comes to the water's edge to meet us. Even out here in the sticks, football is a common language, it seems. The familiarity of it is strangely comforting.

"Why are you here?" inquires young Liverpool frankly, demonstrating a surprisingly good grasp of English.

He stands on one foot, propping himself up with a short stick, and scratches at a scabby knee while mucus creeps thickly from a nostril. The dogs are snarling, exposing horrible yellowed fangs. The kid beats them back casually and they whimper and retreat, cowed.

"*Dumela. O tsogile?*" (Greetings. Are you well?) "We are lost. Where is your father?" asks Mike.

The boy waves us towards the circle of huts. It's obviously

a gathering point and trading post for passing fishermen and travellers, a place where people come and go in their flat-bottomed, wooden *mekoro* as they ply the waterways of the Okavango Delta. In this watery environment there is no other mode of transport: everything is moved by boat, even household goods and small livestock. Nylon fishing nets drape from wooden frames between the trees and the cloying stench of drying fish hangs heavily in the air. Chickens scratch energetically at the bare swept earth between the dwellings. There is a *cuca* here, a small shop made of corrugated iron and palm fronds. Its rough-hewn wooden shelves are laden with essentials: sunflower oil, sugar, *mealie* meal, salt, tins of Lucky Star pilchards, tobacco and quart bottles of warm St. Louis Lager.

Young Liverpool leads us to a wiry, serious-looking man seated, pipe in hand, on a low wooden stool near a communal fire. We make deference, attempting the *Setswana* greeting. He rises and greets us doubtfully, extending a gnarled hand. At first he speaks to us in "*fanakalo*" but then he switches to halting English.

"*Dumela, bo rra.*" (Greetings, men.) "Where are you going?"

"Maun, *rra*. We need to be there by Saturday. We have six days. But it is difficult to find the way," we reply.

He gestures with open contempt at our canoes.

"These boats? Six days? You cannot. You need *mekoro*."

"Yes, um, we need a guide. Do you know who can take us to Maun?" I ask him.

He frowns and slowly shakes his grizzled head.

"You cannot manage. I have come from there. Today, I arrived. In my *makoro*, five days – he holds up five fingers – but in your boats, many days. Too many. In your boat, it is difficult. And there are many hippos."

We shift uneasily. We haven't seen any hippos yet but we've heard them grunting in the sheltered ponds we have paddled by. They are our biggest fear. And we *must* get to Maun by Saturday at the latest. Pat is there waiting for us and we still have to make the long drive back to Durban. It's going to be nip and tuck getting back to work on time.

"Can you take us *rra*?" I venture.

I don't like the sound of the pleading in my voice as I ask him, but we only have one roll of the dice. He seems hesitant. After all, he's just arrived. What would induce him to go all the way back with four naïve young men in tow? Well, money, I suppose. Money is a universal lubricant.

"Of course, we will pay you," I say hastily. "We will pay you to take us to Maun."

We're making a plan. We're young, we have no restraints and we're making a plan. The old man looks at the declining sun, looks again at our boats, looks at the four of us, semi-bearded, grubby, but obviously fit and strong. He makes up his mind.

"I will take you to Delta Camp. But it is many days. From there, you go alone. My name, it is Zobra. I will need food. We will go soon. Today."

We quickly agree a price: it's most of the *pula*, the local currency, that we can muster, but this is a seller's market. He rises and walks over to the cuca, saying something rapidly to the shop-keeper. Young Liverpool is summoned and despatched to the *makoro*, staggering under the weight of a bag of *mealie* meal, some tea and sugar, a handful of onions and a few tins of fish. We pay for the provisions, buy some fish for ourselves, and order some warm beer too, which we drink standing right there to celebrate our success. Zobra has disappeared among the houses, presumably collecting his needs and saying his goodbyes. We begin to fret: time is of the essence. But then he reappears, ominously carrying a rusted old rifle. I hope he doesn't have to use it: it looks like it would explode in his hands. He jerks a chin at the boats.

"*Samaya bo rra*." (Come. We go, men.)

Standing tall in the stern, he backs his dugout out into the stream, spins it easily about, and propels it in a long arc towards the channel, heading south, poling in long, sinuous, deliberate strokes, energy efficient, as it's been done in the Delta since time immemorial. He is a master of his craft. Literally. The four of us clamber keenly into our canoes, and fall in line astern. We feel triumphant, and it reflects in our eagerness as we paddle strongly across the quiet, creeping pond, little eddies swirling away from our blades.

The water flows swiftly in the channel and we make grand progress at first. This is what we envisioned: cruising, floating down the river, taking photographs, enjoying leisurely fish lunches, a big cheerful fire at night. Bliss. But almost immediately Zobra leaves this glorious channel, nosing his dugout through a small gap in the flanking reeds. We dutifully follow but we don't like the view that unfolds before us: a wide, shallow floodplain with swathes of tall grass protruding through the surface, and no clean route. The grass tugs at our boats, impeding us, and the paddles catch on the floating vegetation. This causes the canoes to tilt and water to slop over the gunwales, wetting our kit on the floor of the canoe and dampening the foodstuffs.

But then it becomes clear: he's heading for a palm-fringed island nearby. This makes sense. The hour is late and it is time to make camp. Hippos are starting to become active. Right, everyone out. Let's make a fire, drink some more beer, break out the tinned fish. This is great!

"*Robala sentlè*" (Sleep well), says Zobra as he unfolds his blankets after dinner.

But we sleep fretfully. Tiny red ants are active by night on the island and we are woken by the sensation of our scalps creeping. The ants are everywhere, in our hair, our food, our sleeping bags. They are impossible to remove in the pure darkness. Zobra sleeps on, wrapped in his blankets, apparently impervious. In the morning Mike discovers a black leech attached to the underside of his foot, swollen, engorged and disgusting. It has been feasting there all night. He takes an ember and burns it off with the greatest sangfroid.

The old man is up early, talking to himself, hardly looking at us, poking at the fire, making *motogo*, a simple *mealie* meal porridge. It's a stodgy mix of corn flour, water, salt and lots of sugar, and looks vastly unappetising. He offers us some, lumped on an old wooden spoon, but we decline, sticking with our Provitas and peanut butter, and several cups of sweet tea. Before the sun has had time to warm us the fire has been doused and we are back in the boats.

Zobra punts out through the shallows again, avoiding the channel. A short-cut perhaps? But he just keeps poling through the water lilies, steering clear of deep water. It's very hard work in our boats, but we soldier on, scaring up African Jacanas and other still-water birds and taking delight in the little multi-coloured Reed Frogs that plop into our laps as we force our way through overhanging reed-passages. There's fishing to be done in these knee-deep waters, and we'd love to be able to stop and hook out a juicy bream. But Zobra is merciless: he keeps moving, poling in that steady rhythm of his, hour after hour, never tiring, metronomic, indefatigable. It's impressive to see. In our canoes the progress seems so slow, the water so shallow that sometimes we have to get out and push the boats. It's exhausting and we begin to yawn with fatigue. The copper sun beats relentlessly down. We never stop. On and on. Eventually my patience wears thin, and I gather the temerity to question our saviour.

"Zobra. Zobra! Hang on a bit! Why are we going through the shallow water? Let's go back to the deep channel: it's faster. It's better!"

Do guardian angels really need to explain? Zobra gives me a long, patient, considering look. These young fellows know nothing, he's thinking. It's amazing they even got as far as Seronga.

"It is dangerous," he says flatly.

He's not one to communicate much. But the whole *place* is dangerous, I think. That's partly why we are here. It would be really nice to make some good deep-water progress towards Maun, though.

"*Ja*, but can't we just take the channel for a while?" I ask deferentially.

We're tired and very hungry indeed: our peanut butter is finished and the Provitas are mushy. Zobra stops poling. His *makoro* drifts to a stop. For a short time he looks down at the four of us as we float there expectantly. I feel like a naughty child, like Oliver Twist asking for more. Zobra's tone is unexpectedly forbearing, as that of a mentor to an errant child.

"I went to the mines in Johannesburg. The place we call Egoli. For work. When I was a young man, like you. Many of us did this. It was dangerous work, in the darkness, underground. Many people were injured, some people died. After that work, I came back to Seronga to help my father at the cattle-post. Also for fishing with the nets. But here it is also dangerous."

He removes his soiled old T-shirt, and points at his right upper-arm and shoulder. We gasp. They are a mass of scar tissue, old lacerated flesh that has healed into a maze of lines and furrows, a mangled mess of muscle and sinew. There is a collective intake of breath, then stunned silence. It looks awful.

"You see. Crocodile. I was fishing in the deep water, the channel, with the nets, standing and throwing, standing and throwing, and then suddenly – he claps his hands loudly for effect – *Munna!* (Guys!) Out of the water, a big crocodile, bigger than me, and it took me by the arm and pulled me into the water. One shot!"

Zobra has our undivided attention: it's impossible not to stare. He's animated, reliving the episode, his arms wide and his face alive.

"I was under the water for a long time. Hey! And the crocodile was turning over and over, spinning, trying to break my arm off. And there was blood in the water. Too much blood. I thought I was dead. Then the crocodile let go. I do not know why. I came to the top of the water and my *makoro* was still there and I got in. I managed."

He has hammered this nail deep and true and we take his point. But he continues.

"Another fisherman was nearby and he heard me shouting and he came quickly and put his shirt on the bleeding. And from the village they took me to the clinic and put bandages and gave me many tablets and then later I was all right."

Zobra turns away, and puts his shirt back on. The scars are hideous and we're glad not to have to look at them anymore.

"We stay in the shallow water," he says serenely, picking up his *ngashi* and gliding away.

We look at each other. Mike raises an ironic eyebrow. There are no more questions. On we go, without a break, the pace unrelenting.

It takes us a further three days just to reach Delta Camp but from there, Zobra assures us, all we have to do is follow the Boro river – the clear, shallow and winding Boro river – for another two days until we reach Maun. It looks like we're going to make it. Only just.

At the landing stage, we pay Zobra all our money, more than we had agreed to. We feel sad to say goodbye, strangely abandoned.

He leans on his *ngashi* and raises a cautionary finger.

"*Sala sentle.* (Goodbye.) Do not go in the deep water," he says quietly.

And for the first time since we have met him, Zobra smiles.

EPILOGUE

I wrote the first draft of this book in fifty days, sitting at a kitchen table in Richmond, south-west London in the winter of 2014/15, as the airliners droned overhead, wheels down, on short-finals into Heathrow. In every paragraph, and every line, with every word, I was in Africa: the urban world outside the narrow windows ceased to exist. The power of memory and imagination was brought home to me, and I was reminded that this is what an Africa safari does to people: it is a time vacuum of colour and excitement that removes them from the normal routines of their lives. The essential and elemental rawness of the wilderness occupies you fully when you go to Africa. It enters deep into your soul, and never lets go. Africa bites! It changes your state. For all of humankind, Africa is home: you may think you're visiting it, but actually it's where we all came from in the first place. That's why it feels so welcoming, and warm; that's why it is hard to leave.

Home. These days I live in two hemispheres, enjoying the benefits of both. Many clients find this odd. Surely, they ask, you must miss waking up to the dawn chorus of the bush? I do. I miss it every single day when I am in the UK. But Africa is only an eleven-hour overnight flight away, and I return many times a year to lead safaris. It's a wonderful new world, this age of internet and jet travel and immediate communications, and I embrace it enthusiastically. It allows me to lead a new kind of life, to be more than the sum of my parts.

I loved writing these twenty-five stories, and as I did, I remembered how many more I have to tell. So I am delighted to say that *Africa Bites Twice: tales from the rough edge of Africa* is an inevitable result of this first volume. I hope you enjoyed reading them: there are plenty more to come. You may even find that you're in one of them! Africa awaits!

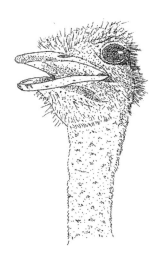

GLOSSARY

Aapjas: heavy army-issue coat (Afrikaans)

Abseil: to descend a cliff face on a rope using a mechanical device as a safety brake (also, rappel)

Acacia: Latin generic name for many species of a thorny tree very common across Africa

Aestivating: when an animal lies in a state of torpor awaiting wetter environmental conditions

Afrikaans: one of the languages of South Africa, originating mainly from Dutch

Bakkie: small pick-up truck (Afrikaans)

Boet: brother (Afrikaans). Used also to denote a good friend

Braai: barbeque (Afrikaans)

Buffel: military troop-carrying vehicle (Afrikaans for buffalo)

Bwana mkubwa: Big chief (kiSwahili)

Checked: saw/observed (colloquial South African English)

China: friend (colloquial South African English)

Click: kilometre (also 'kay')

Coppery-tailed Coucal: a medium-sized bird that occurs in reed and papyrus beds in the Okavango Delta

Cuca: small rural shop made of sheets of corrugated iron and wood

Dagga boy: old male buffalo who likes to wallow in cooling mud (*dhaga* = mud in Zulu)

Damaraland: the traditional territory of the Damara people of north-western Namibia

Damara-Nama: common language of the Damara and Nama peoples of Namibia

Dissed: put down (originally, dismissed)

Dixie: aluminium eating vessel (army-issue)

Drift: road crossing over a shallow river

Dubbeltjies: Devil-thorn creepers (Afrikaans)

Egoli: African colloquialism for Johannesburg (literally, 'Place of Gold')

Fanakalo: a polyglot language comprised of Zulu, English and Afrikaans devised as a lingua franca on the South African mines

Flatdog: colloquialism for crocodile

Greytown: small country village in KwaZulu-Natal Province, South Africa

Gum trees: *Eucalyptus* species from Australia, grown commercially for timber

Himba: correctly, OvaHimba. A migratory pastoral tribe of northern Namibia and southern Angola

Ixopo: small country village in KwaZulu-Natal Province, South Africa

Ja: yes (Afrikaans: commonly used by South Africans of all races)

Jislaaik: expression of alarm (Afrikaans)

Kay: kilometre (also 'click')

Kobas: a squat mountain tree typical of rocky places in Namibia

Ko ko: morning greeting (Setswana)

Kraal: enclosure for stock in an African homestead (Afrikaans)

Kruger National Park: South Africa's largest and most famous National Park

Kunene river: a wild frontier river between Namibia and Angola

Kweek: spiky grass, called Couch, common across Africa (Afrikaans)

Lekgoa: white person (Setswana)

Lekker: great/nice (Afrikaans: commonly also used by English-speaking South Africans)

Lowveld: north-eastern South Africa, a place of many private game reserves and the Kruger National Park (literally, low lying bush savannah)

Mahango: pearl millet, the staple crop of the Owambo people

Makoro (pl: mekoro): traditional shallow-draughted wooden dugout canoe used in the Okavango Delta

Mealie meal: maize/corn, ground into flour

Mopane: characteristic tree of dry areas of southern Africa

Munna: men (Setswana)

Nama: a tribal grouping, mostly in southern Namibia

Ngashi: long forked stick used to pole a makoro in the shallow waters of the Okavango Delta in north-central Botswana

Oliphant: SADF battle tank (Afrikaans, meaning 'elephant')

Omurambas: low-lying areas that fill with water when the annual flood comes

Owamboland: the traditional territory of the Owambo people of northern Namibia and southern Angola. (The Owambo people speak oshiWambo)

Paraat: over-zealous soldier, eager to please his commanding officers (Afrikaans)

Paraglider: a parachute-like canopy attached by a harness to a person that allows the pilot to glide after taking off from a height

PB (plaaslike bevolking): local population (Afrikaans)

Pikstel: army-issue cutlery set (Afrikaans)

Pula: the currency of Botswana. Also the word for rain, and used as a greeting

Ratpack: daily ration pack for soldiers

Ringbolt: a metal ring hammered into the rock for the secure attachment of a rope

Rusks: traditional South African dried out biscuit or bread

SADF: South African Defence Force

Schadenfreude: pleasure derived from the misfortunes of others (German)

Setswana/Motswana/Batswana: the language, a person (sing.), the people (pl.) of the country of Botswana

Sit Rep: military abbreviation for 'situation report'

Spoor: tracks (Afrikaans)

Tiffy: a technician (short for 'artificer')

Torra: local Damara-Nama name for an area of north-western Namibia. Describes the local red volcanic pillow lava that is common in the area

Vasbyt: an extremely demanding physical and mental challenge which trainee officers in the SADF have to complete in order to prove their mettle (Afrikaans)

Veld: southern African savannah (Afrikaans)

Velskoene: traditional leather every-day shoes (Afrikaans)

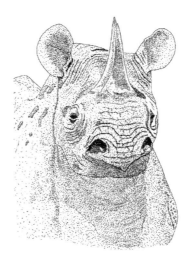

ABOUT THE AUTHOR

Lloyd Camp is a safari itinerary specialist, guide and guide trainer who grew up in South Africa and has been leading eco-tourism trips to the great wildlife destinations of Africa, including Namibia, Botswana, Zimbabwe, Zambia, Tanzania, Rwanda, Uganda and South Africa since 1992. He started his guiding career in the South African *lowveld* before moving to Botswana where he and his wife Sue managed several safari lodges. They subsequently moved to Namibia where Lloyd established a staff training division for a large safari company, and established a reputation as a specialist guide, guide trainer and a leader of bespoke walking safaris.

Lloyd and Sue currently live in London, from where he operates his specialist guiding business, Lloyd Camp Consulting Africa, in association with the Magalena Corporation.

In his spare time he likes to look at wild creatures, climb mountains, run marathons, paddle kayaks and go for very long walks. He claims that just because he likes to wander, it doesn't mean that he is lost.

45405647R00121

Made in the USA
Lexington, KY
26 September 2015